'Box On'

'Box On'

THE AUTOBIOGRAPHY OF

HARRY GIBBS

as told to John Morris

PELHAM BOOKS

First published in Great Britain by
Pelham Books Ltd
44 Bedford Square
London WC1B 3DU
1981

British Library Cataloguing in Publication Data

Gibbs, Harry
    Box on
    I. Gibbs, Harry
    1. Title
    796.8'3'0924   GV1137.3

ISBN 0 7207 1364 1

Printed and bound in Great Britain by
Billing & Sons Ltd, Guildford,
London and Worcester

Contents

	List of Illustrations	7
1	The Bermondsey Boy	9
2	On With the Gloves	21
3	War — and a Long Road Home	30
4	A Girl With My Tea	44
5	My Corinthians	52
6	'Old Toffee' in Charge	61
7	Time to Make Decisions	72
8	A Cold Stare for Ali	84
9	Sorry Henry — But I was in Charge	92
10	Trouble With the Rota	104
11	A Gathering of Champions	113
12	You Have to Be the Guv'nor	127
13	It's Always Great to Come Home	137
14	Old Big 'Ed	151

Illustrations

Between pages 96 and 97

Nellie and the redoubtable Gus
All smiles on repatriation day
Culture, too, with Shakespeare
Spot the British champions
Family group — with wife Phyllis and daughter Sheila
Proud Grandad with Nicola and Matthew
'What am I bid?'
Giving a warning to John H. Stracey
Gangway for a referee
Counting out Brian London against Muhammad Ali
Summit meeting in Zambia
Joe Bugner and Joe Frazier battle it out
Enough is quite enough
'Now wait just a moment, lads'
In the ring with Mark Rowe
Dave 'Boy' Green against John H. Stracey
Welshman Brian Curvis and the great Emile Griffith
'Whoops, hold up Hedgemon'
Billy Walker in trouble against Jack Bodell
'The winner' — Alan Rudkin's arm is raised
'Nine and out' — Lennie 'The Lion' Williams against
　　Frankie Taylor

1

The Bermondsey Boy

The funeral carriages were drawn up outside 20 Alscot Road, Bermondsey, the horsedrawn hearse led the cortège on a winter's day. But the mourners were forced to wait in a chill wind while two grubby boys, one in his best Sunday suit, were removed from beneath the horses' hooves where they had rolled, locked in combat.

Young Henry William Gibbs was settling a dispute the way so many were settled in those precarious days between the wars, but he had chosen the wrong moment, of course. It was the talk of the street — what a disgrace to be fighting as my granny's funeral procession waited to move off. I was in hot water again but that was nothing new and, in any case, Joey Francis had got in and killed someone's racing pigeons and that caused a row amongst the kids down the street. All it earned me was a belting from Joey who was a big lad and a bit better than me, and another from my Dad for scandalising the neighbourhood.

In those days the Gibbs family was well known in Bermondsey — after all there were enough of us, and they were hard times for the Gibbs just as they were for so many other families who did really live on the breadline, whatever folk today may say about recessions as they sit back watching their colour television sets. I suppose to most people Bermondsey simply means a few acres of London dockland south of the Thames, a bit down at heel but soon left behind as you move away from the river. To me it has always meant home, wonderful warm people and so many memories I doubt if I shall remember half the things I want to, or the people either . . . although I'll do my best.

These days I jet around the world to referee or judge world title fights in a way I could never possibly have dreamt of as a kid. Then, Bermondsey was my world, the battleground for people whose main concern was survival but who still found time to enjoy themselves in a community that looked after its own as well as it could and, I am sure, as well as any in times when there was still real poverty.

If I found time for sporting ambitions as a lad I saw myself as a famous footballer, although using the fists was second nature to Bermondsey boys. After all, footballs and football boots cost money but fists cost nothing and all boys like to fight, don't they? Certainly it never crossed my mind that one day I would be refereeing boxing in exotic places because I had never heard of most of them then. Bermondsey had a reputation as a tough area and I would be less than fair if I did not admit that it could be pretty violent, but if we had a stand-up fight it was always with the fists. The fellow who kicked was a coward and might be sent to Coventry, while knives were unheard-of.

My father Arthur Frederick Gibbs, known to all and sundry as 'Gussy', was a naval man who served eighteen years with the fleet right through the Great War. According to family legend, when he was fourteen he sailed round The Horn as a galley boy on a sailing ship and then he joined the Royal Navy as a stoker. In our front room I'll always remember the picture we had of 'The Blucher' which Dad always claimed was sunk by his ship 'The Indomitable' at the battle of the Dogger Bank. Apparently the admiral had the flags run out to say 'Well done, the Black Squad of 'The Indomitable'. That was a pat on the back for the stokers, of course, and our picture was of the German ship on the way down, with all the sailors clinging to it as the vessel turned over. Not the happiest of pictures when you think about it, but Dad was as proud as punch of it.

Father came originally from Custom House while mother's family, the Slatchers, were from Northampton. Helen Leticia, known as Nellie, was as much a character in her own way as Dad and the pair of them did a good job raising a brood of seven of us in conditions that would daunt a great many today. There were five boys and I was fourth in line after Arthur, the eldest who is retired and living in Bermondsey, Ted, who was four years older than me and died in 1977 and Sid, who is two years my senior. Philip, the last one out of the pot, is a foreman plumber and lives in Aveley. I had two sisters: Kathleen who married a fighter, Johnny Allen — very much one of the Bermondsey boxing fraternity — and Lil who went to live in Liverpool and over the years has lost touch with the family.

After the 1914-18 war Dad went to work in the docks, like many of his family over in the East End, and he gave me my first lessons in acting as a referee. In our street it was the favourite sport on a Friday night for a man to give his wife a right-hander when she wanted the wages and Gussy Gibbs was the peacemaker. They used to come and knock at our door and over Dad would go to square up the warring couple. He was a big man with a persuasive manner and without any doubt they listened to him because he was well loved and respected.

However, I can't really claim that this set me on the road to being a referee because I was mad on football at that time. Not that father objected to that; he had played in goal for the Navy and after they defeated the Army 1-0 at Portsmouth in 1919 they presented him with the ball. While he was serving he had been allowed to play a bit of professional football, notably, I think, for Chatham. Father influenced me in many ways and I realise this more now, looking back, than I ever did at the time. He was a very fair man, very red, white and blue, and I suppose in many ways a real Conservative which a great many of his

Bermondsey neighbours were not, as you can imagine.

When I was born the family were living in Larnica Street but my only memories are of Alscot Road, first at number 20 and then at number 50 after the war because number 20 was bombed out during the years I was away, a very reluctant prisoner-of-war for more than five years. Our place was simply one of an ordinary terraced row and, like so many others in the neighbourhood, it had to house far too many people. My gran lived downstairs with two of her sons and a daughter, while we were all upstairs in three rooms, seven of us kids with mother and dad as well.

We used to call our bedroom the anteroom and we relied just on a fishtailed jet to see by because Dad could not afford a proper gas mantle when we were all young. The four of us lads used to sleep 'top and tail' in one big bed, and that caused a few rumpuses. Arthur, the eldest, had already started work and was taking a keen interest in his appearance with the ladies in mind. One night there was a terrible scene when Sid swung out with a foot and opened a sizable scratch down Arthur's face with his toe-nails. Arthur demanded instant correction, fetched the scissors from downstairs and made certain Sid's nails were cut right back before he tried to go back to sleep.

Arthur was the one who, I reckon, could have been a world champion if he had wished. He would fight at the drop of a hat and was very much the guv'nor among the local kids. He was named after father and down the street everyone knew he was the boss. He finished up in the Navy during the war while Sid was in the Eighth Army. Phil was too young and Ted was not well enough to go in. Poor old Ted always had a weak heart but he took a lot from father while we were all away. 'You should be where your brothers are' father would say. Ted went up to volunteer and was chucked out because he could not pass the medical, but that did not stop father leading him a dog's life through the war.

When we were kids Dad was a foreman, first at New Fresh Wharf when it belonged to Lord John Neill and then over at Jarl Wharf. He used to earn around 14s 6d a day and each night the men were paid off in a pub. The Labour Master, who had set them on in the morning, would be sitting there and the odd sixpence from each man's money went to him. If a man did not give the Labour Master something there was a more than even chance he would not be going to work the next morning because it was all casual work allocated on a day-to-day basis.

As soon as Dad came in the door Mum would be after him: 'Have you been drinking?' Dad may well have had a few pints (only 4d in those days) but he would always say much the same: 'Before you start Nell, your money's in my waistcoat pocket.' He used to give her 11 bob out of his money, but, of course, there were a good many days when there was no work at all. The dockers were allowed to carry their unemployment benefit over for weeks but if they did three days work in any one week they did not receive the benefit. I remember mother having to go round to what we called 'The Bun House' for a means test, and if they thought you had a case they gave you bread, or rather a coupon to go and get it. All round we had it rough, but no more so than just about every other family round us.

There may be people these days who turn up their noses at charity organisations and people who help others in need, but we were glad of them I can tell you. Just as I was grateful to the Salvation Army later when I was just out of the prison camp, so men like old Dr Kedwood stood pretty high with folk in Bermondsey. The Doctor ran the local Central Hall, a chapel man, Methodist or Wesleyan, I forget which, and he helped in the most practical of ways. For instance, he used to give free boots away to kids who were picked out at school. I remember being handed a pair and a little sailor's top. I had great holes in the bottom of my old boots and because we could not afford to have them soled I was relying on pieces of cardboard pushed down inside.

Every Christmas the Doctor handed out turkeys, although not simply to anyone who happened to be passing — he gave them to the women who attended his mid-week services during the year. He was no fool either, because they had to have a star marked in a little record book so that he knew they had been among the faithful and deserved his turkey. Catholics, Protestants and plenty who did not believe anything in particular used to turn up week after week to be sure of that festive bird. One year something must have gone wrong because there was Dr Kedwood handing out lumps of beef. I'm afraid his congregation did not take it kindly and he was called all sorts of a bachelor's son.

Religion may have played a part in lending us all a helping hand at times, but it never caused us any trouble when we were young. In Bermondsey you often heard someone say he was fighting for the Catholics or the Protestants — but all he meant was which boxing club he belonged to. When I was boxing as a pro I trained at the Fisher Club which is part of the huge Catholic Downside community. I think I was the only Protestant to do so but there was simply no hostility over religion that I can remember in Bermondsey. The first time I ever came across any trouble to do with religion was in the prison camps when the Liverpool lads had a go at the Jocks about Orangemen. Up until then I always thought an Orangeman was a golliwog on a marmalade jar.

Sport played a big part in life for Bermondsey Boys with fighting top of the list for most of us. I remember one lad called Wally Dorney coming round and knocking on our front door. He announced he had come to fight Siddie Gibbs. Now my elder brother was always the diplomat: 'Sorry,' he said, 'I've not got the time just now but our Harry'll fight you.' So out I went to do battle. I was always fighting, always with the knuckles until I started to go to a club and learn properly. I enjoyed it too, but then it was simply the national pastime so far as we were concerned.

Brother Sid may have sent me into the street as his fighting deputy on occasions, but he was the star of the family when it came to sport. He was better than I was at football and a real performer on a cricket pitch. He captained the school teams and could run the 440 yards in 58 seconds, which was good for a lad in the 'thirties. He had just signed on for Blackheath Harriers when the war broke out and upset his track career, just as it upset things for so many of us.

I was always keen on sport. At Junior school in Alexis Street I was a centre-forward but when I moved on to Alma School I became a goalkeeper like father. We won the local Schools' Cup one year and our headmaster, Dr Fisher, bought our outfits for us, even though his own great love was cricket. These days I do not know too much about schools and schoolteachers, but we were looked after by some really dedicated blokes. They gave up a lot of their own time to help us train down in Southwark Park and took a great interest in us. Even so, we sorted out most of our sport for ourselves and naturally it got us into plenty of scrapes.

On one corner not far from Alscot Road was a little clothing shop where mother would parade us every year as regular as clockwork to be rigged out for Christmas. She would spend half-a-crown on each of us for a Japanese-made jersey and tie and a pair of trousers. This particular year I was handed my new outfit and allowed to go out to play wearing it. A definite mistake. Off a gang of us went to The Star, which had been the old vaudeville palace, one of the oldest in London. By then it had changed to showing pictures and we would wait round the corner for half-time. As people came out we slipped inside while the doors were open and slid straight into the toilets. As soon as the lights went down again in we walked to take a seat, only on this occasion I was spotted and an attendant grabbed me, clutching onto the collar of my brand new Japanese job. As I ran for it the collar came off in his hand, and that meant a good hiding when I finally dared to go home.

I suppose it was a pretty small world but that did not worry us in the slightest because it was all we knew, and we found plenty of fun around. In Bermondsey there was always a wealth of community spirit and I am sure there still is, despite all the changes. In the evenings the men all got together and had a few pints, always providing they could afford it. Most of them were dockers but we had some leather works, a glue factory and a scent works, which meant there were some pretty weird perfumes wafting over Bermondsey in those days.

On summer evenings most people sat outside whenever the weather was fine enough. It helped the social whirl I suppose, but that was not the reason why we didn't want to go upstairs. In many a house the Red Army was on the march — that is what we used to call the steam tugs, otherwise the bugs. When they were marching about in the hot weather we never used to get a lot of sleep.

As kids we couldn't hop on a bus or the tube and go up West. Our biggest thrill was to go under the river through Rotherhithe Tunnel and climb up the stairway to see the ships. Or else we would go over Tower Bridge or down to the wharves where the peanuts came in. They weren't baked and the dockers pushing them on trucks would make sure we could grab handfuls of nuts. My own biggest joy was to go down Tower Bridge Road with my mother on a Saturday night. The butchers on the stalls kept open and auctioned off their H-bones of beef, which was the cheapest cut of meat in those days. You can't get anything similar now, and I suppose it would cost a lot of money if you could. I used to carry the bag and on the way back mother often took me into a pie and eel shop called Mansie's. I sat there proudly and tucked into a pie and a pen'uth before carrying the bag back home. That was providing Dad was in work and we could afford the trip: work was scarce, the dockers were not registered and there was no Dock Labour Board then.

You read a lot about the villains in the East End and in South East London too, but I have few memories of real trouble with the police although we had a few brushes with the law and we respected the local coppers. We all knew the Bermondsey policemen by name and when they came plodding past to find more than a couple of you talking on the pavement, they soon warned you to move out of the road. If you were still there when they came back they reached out to put their macs round your ears — and you ran for your life if you had any sense.

There was one policeman we called 'Swanee', because of his Adam's apple I think, and one day when I was climbing on the Town Hall railings he came past with a Sergeant Thackeray. When I saw them coming I called out 'Swanee River, Swanee River' and ran for it. We had the idea that policemen never ran. Well this one did and he very quickly caught up with me. I clung to the railings while he clipped me round the ear with his gloves. I was only a little lad and so frightened and surprised by this time that while he was clipping me I was weeing my shorts in terror. Finally I ran home to tell my Dad, and received another walloping.

It was not very often that one of my contemporaries was carted off to court, except for serious crimes of course. A favourite sport of ours was to go down Southwark Park Road or Tower Bridge Road and nick an apple off a stall. If they caught you and handed you over to a copper, justice was instant. They sorted it out there and then and didn't take your character away by dragging you off to court — and once warned not many of us did it again. I wonder how many cases today could be sorted out as quickly if you left it to the police to administer justice on the spot.

We spent a lot of time climbing and football in the street was also a regular game. Of course, it was not nearly so dangerous then because the traffic was mainly horses and carts with a few lorries with solid rubber tyres thrown in. Then there were the trams, and they figured in a special treat for those of us who turned up to Dr Kedwood's Sunday School. On the appointed afternoon a spruced-up crowd of us would climb onto the tram for a trip through Lewisham to Catford and on to Peter Pan's Playground at Southend Ponds. It seemed like miles and miles to us, but I doubt if it was more than four in fact. Once a year we made a longer expedition when we set off on the dockers' outing. It was always to Theydon Bois near Epping, which is in Essex not far from where I live now. On the charabanc each child was handed 'thru'pence' and your mother sewed your ticket onto your jersey to make certain it was not lost before the ride back.

Just once a year, too, came the opportunity for a real holiday, or at least what passed for one for most of us. There were two chances. Firstly the schools ran what was called a Country Holiday Fund and each week the mums sent in 6d. Then in the summer people living in the country took children in for a holiday and the fund money paid the fares. For the Gibbs family that was out — mother would have been hard put to find 6d a week for seven. But there was still the hopping, and the hop fields proved an adventure playground for me and many like me.

The hop farmers down in Kent always used Cockney labour to pick their crop for them and each year half Bermondsey would join the invasion. The procedure was to write to the farmers and then get back what was known as the first hopping letter which engaged you. Then you had to wait for the second hopping letter which told you that you were sure of employment and to which farm your family would be going. At school the big topic for weeks was 'Have you got your second hopping letter yet?'

Apart from the fun of it all and the change of scenery, the trip had a particular attraction for the school kids. The hop-picking season started at the end of August and for those chosen it meant an extra month away from school on the end of the summer break. We went as a rule to Wickham's Farm near Goudhurst and on the great morning of the exodus we were all up at 3am. It seemed as if the whole borough was on the move as the mothers and children gathered with their hopping carts. The fathers, of course, remained at home to carry on working in the docks, or wherever. The carts, incidentally, were contraptions on four wheels, pram wheels usually with a box fixed on top into which were piled all the pots and pans we would need in Kent.

The emigration wound down Tooley Street and on to London Bridge station. Everyone kept a sharp eye for the ticket collector to turn his head and your mum would order 'Quick, nip through there', so as to save a half fare. The farmers laid on special trains, I think, and down at Marden the farm wagons would be waiting. The hopping carts were loaded in and it was off to the hop fields.

The contrast between Bermondsey and the farms was from one extreme to the other, but there was little luxury waiting, although I am sure none of us worried in the slightest. We were housed in rows of special huts rather like Nissen huts, and everyone was handed a pile of faggots of brushwood. These made up your bed once you had piled straw on top of them. No sooner had we arrived than all the kids were off, up to the banks of the River Medway. This was a totally different proposition from Old Father Thames as it runs through the London Docks, and we went armed with string and bent pin in the traditional quest for fish.

We must have looked a strange bunch, too, because before the trip all the boys were sent for a hopping haircut, which meant a very close crop. It cost 4d and all the barber did was take just about the whole lot off. On our feet we wore clogs which our mothers bought for us specially. They were much the same as the clogs used in the lime pits in Bermondsey but with the metal parts taken off to make them real wooden clogs.

The big sport was scrumping and in the heart of Kent you had the choice of some of the best apples in the world. The farmers had to put up with it, but not without a battle at times; security methods were pretty basic and once again justice was instant. They often had blokes on patrol with double-barrelled shotguns and they didn't hesitate to give us a peppering. Even then we still had plenty of those apples.

In the mornings we went into the fields with the women to start helping with the hops, but we pretty soon ran off to play until the lolly man came round. He was the fellow who shouted out 'Lolly, lolly' as he came round selling ha'penny sherbert dabs. Back you would go to persuade your mum to buy you one, and she used it as a bribe to get you back working for just a bit longer.

Our near neighbours in the hop fields were the gypsies and they were artists when it came to catching rabbits. At night they often sent up a few for the pickers and these went into what we called the hopping pot and I've never tasted such delicious stews as we had on those hopping holidays. I've often told my wife Phyllis about them and said she can't cook like my mother used to. But she is right when she says, 'When you were kids you were always hungry and so it tasted better, especially down in the hop fields.'

2

On With the Gloves

After my early adventures street fighting I finally reached the magic age of eleven years, and that meant I was old enough to join the Oxford and Bermondsey Boys' Clubs, a series of establishments that must be owed a vast debt by generations of lads in Bermondsey.

Among the many activities now open to me was boxing, with proper instruction by men who knew the job, and it was not very long before I discovered that brute force and ignorance led to pain and anguish if used against a boy who had been taught to use his fists properly. No doubt it was a valuable lesson at the time because the first opportunity that came along I jumped up into the ring to show what I could do. I sparred with a lad called Tom Berryman and he knocked the living daylights out of me — certainly it felt that way. But I kept going and I think Charles Blasdell, one of the men who ran the clubs and later became a great influence on me, took a liking to me because I didn't scream about it and just tried as hard as I could.

Men like Charlie Blasdell did wonderful work but the man who really shook up Bermondsey was Dr John Stansfield. He it was who founded the Stansfield Oxford and Bermondsey Clubs and first taught boxing to local lads by pushing furniture to one side in his surgery. He had a special rallying cry for Oxford undergraduates to persuade them to spend their holidays assisting him: 'Come to Bermondsey and be crucified!' he would tell them. I know we were tough, but not quite that tough and a lot of us have good reason to be grateful to the students who answered the doctor's call.

In all there were five clubs and as soon as you reached the age of eleven you could join the 'minors'. Once I was able to clutch my 3d a week and go along to enrol, my first club was called The Decima, later renamed The Hertford. The Gordon was named after Gordon Stansfield, the doctor's son who drowned in the River Irrewaddy trying to rescue an Indian, and then there were the Dockhead Club, the Canterbury Club and The Old Boys Club for the over eighteens. I hope I have got the names correct, and if I haven't I shall hear about it pretty smartly because I am still in close touch both with the clubs and many friends in Bermondsey.

Charlie Blasdell lives in Sevenoaks now and we still keep in contact. I shall always remember the time he handed me a three-week suspension — quite a heavy punishment from him — after a crowd of us had been caught smoking while we were out running the Thames bridges, a popular activity for club lads at the time. We were hauled up for judgment and suspended, but before the sentence expired we were summoned back. Blasdell cancelled the rest of the suspension and told us: 'You may come back at once. The clubs are open for boys like you, that's the idea of it and I won't keep you out any longer.'

Other men I recall helping out included people like Sir Reginald Goodwin, Peter Marinden, Hubert Secerton and Capt Alex Patterson, who has been in charge of Her Majesty's Prisons for the Home Office. They taught us all kind of things, with a touch of non-sectarian religion thrown in. If we were in the club at eight in the evening we had to stay on for what was called chapel, a short club service at 9pm.

Despite my early setback with the gloves on, I took to boxing like the proverbial duck to water, abandoned my football daydreams and switched to seeing myself as the heavyweight champion of the world. I was turning into a pretty big lad too and because I was growing so much I was allowed to train with the Old Boys.

When I was 15 I won the Sid Smith Cup awarded to the best junior. It was a proud moment and I've still got the medal that went with the trophy. Sid Smith I remember well because he had the scales in Southwark Park Road where he guessed your weight before you climbed on, but in fact he had been one of Bermondsey's heroes before the First War. In 1913 he won the world flyweight championship by outpointing Eugène Criqui in Paris over 20 rounds, and became the first man to be listed as world champion at this weight in the official records. He held his title for less than two months before being knocked out in London by Bill Ladbury.

A leading light on the Old Boys boxing scene was Bob Marriott who won the national amateur title twice before the 1914-18 War. After the war was over he turned professional and won the British lightweight title after only a couple of fights. He took the title on a 10th round disqualification against Johnny Summers in the first title fight at the weight after the war, but for some reason never defended it.

Bob was a Bermondsey hero, particularly for the Protestants, just as Joe Rolfe was for the Fisher Club and the Catholics, but the man who really taught me was Joe Gogay. Joe was a magnificent figure of a man and just before the Second War, when Hitler was using his Strength and Joy movement for publicity, Joe was one of those picked out to visit Portugal as a typical example of British sportsmen.

Moving up through the weights as a promising young boxer coincided, of course, with leaving schooldays behind and starting the hunt for a job. I did not follow so many of the family into the docks until I came back from the war and nor did I join the Regular Army like quite a few of my mates. When they left school and found work difficult to find and the Depression lingering on around South East London, they lied about their age and signed on for the

King's Shilling, as they called it then. Off they went to far-away places like the North West Frontier of India and some were away for five years and more. We used to kid them when they came home on embarkation leave, all smart in their brand new uniforms, 'You only joined up to get a suit to wear on Sundays'.

I was never tempted and when it came to jobs I was very lucky. After I left school I went for a job as a vanboy for Elizabeth Lazenbys, which is now Cross & Blackwell, and there were five of us with applications in. I got the job and stayed there until they went motorised. They kept me on and offered me a job in the factory, but I didn't fancy that. I went on to try all sorts of jobs, I even started to learn French polishing at one stage, and just before the war started I landed my first job in the docks, at Hays Wharf. I joined their maintenance staff and the only reason I was given the job was because I was going to box for their firm's club. I never did, though. The war began and off I went at once.

My father died of lung cancer within a year of the war ending and I took his dock brief, that is I took on his dock number, and have been in the docks ever since, although that is a story for later.

At one point when work was scarce one of my friends, George Tucker, was with a leather firm called James Garner, and he helped me to find a job in their lime pits, which was hard and mucky work I can tell you. I found myself pairing up with Billy Cottrell, a very useful middleweight from the Fisher Club, and we would spend up to thirteen hours a day dragging sheep pelts out of the pits. We started at six am and worked through to nine at night on some days. We finished up with as much as £4 10s a week, which was a fortune then. With money to spare for once we went down to Petticoat Lane and knocked out the cash on fruit for our mothers and soapy chocolate that they were auctioning on the stalls.

Billy used to kid me when we were unloading salt. He'd get me to put a sack on the back of my neck. He claimed it strengthened the neck muscles but then I found he had loaded me up with his sack as well and was walking along behind with nothing to carry.

In the mid-thirties things started to improve and with a lot more work about, including in the docks, the Gibbs family finances picked up, so much so that Dad was able to lash out on a Murphy wireless, a six-valve set that he had wanted for a long time. It was able to pick up Radio Luxembourg and at the time everybody was mad on Dr Fu Manchu and The Street Singer. Dad had gone down to Mill Pond Bridge and bought the set on the never-never from a Mr Jack Fersht. The fellow who brought it round, a Frenchman, earthed it and it sounded marvellous. All the family were astounded and on the spot he was invited to the Saturday night party to celebrate the new arrival.

The party was soon in full swing. Any old excuse would do for a party and this one was special anyway because the wireless was a new toy. Jimmy McCarthy was singing, his wife Mary played the latest tunes on the piano for him, and Jimmy was wearing a brand new suit and cutting quite a dash. I think he bought it by taking up one of those coupons that enabled you to buy a 50s suit for 42s 6d.

Halfway through the proceedings father went out to go to the toilet and there was the Frenchman, who had started the night as the guest of honour, making amorous advances to one of my sisters. Into the front room he was dragged to face his accusers and then he made a nasty mistake — he pulled out a knife. Quick as a flash my brother-in-law Johnny Allen hit him on the chin. He fell back onto the open fire and was pulled off slightly singed, dazed and with a busted mouth. They picked him up, took him outside and looked around for his bicycle. He had left it propped against a lamp-post, and was plonked astride it and left to come round in his own time.

Back inside Jimmy McCarthy was bemoaning the fate of his 42s 6d suit. As the fight flared up a glass of port had flown all over it, and it was my poor old mum who he never forgave for that. Strangely, we never paid another penny on that wireless. No one came round to collect the instalments, and nor did the Frenchman ever come courting again.

Trouble was rare at our parties though. Certainly we were well able to look after ourselves, but a real old Cockney knees-up was what we enjoyed, not a punch-up. We liked to sing and whether at home or round at the pub we had fun. Those were the days when you made your own entertainment. Television did not exist so far as we were concerned, although the wireless was creating more and more interest.

I was never stuck for entertainment, of course, because boxing kept me busy. I was still an amateur, but for amateurs or professionals Bermondsey was a good place for a fighter to be. The boxers were the local heroes and there were some very good ones still around. Joe Rolfe and Bob Marriott had finished before I was old enough to watch them, and I never saw Tommy Daly fight either. But I did see his brother George and he was brilliant.

As I mentioned before, my sister Kathleen married a pro fighter called Johnny Allen and he fought some good men in his day, including Archie Sexton, father of the Manchester United manager Dave. I suppose you would call Johnny a trial horse, but he was pretty useful. Johnny and many more like him really were hungry fighters. They were the lads who clustered at the back door of the Ring, Blackfriars, which was only just around the corner from Bermondsey, eager for the chance to fight eight or ten rounds just to find the family the price of the Sunday dinner.

Johnny travelled all over and a bloke named Carney, at least I think that was his name, managed him and quite a few others. He would pick them up in his old van and take them off to, say, Rochester Casino just to be announced as next week's attraction.   Mr Carney was something of a showman: he once had Johnny announced as the Champion of the French Canadian lumber camps, and I doubt if he spoke more than a couple of words of French. What it all meant, though, was a lot of hard work and hard fights. It was nothing then to box 15 rounds or even 20 rounds with the winner taking £8 and the loser £6. Not a lot by today's standards, but it was good money for Johnny and his mates.

In 1939 my boxing career took a step forward when I won my novices competition at the Stadium Club in Holborn. Competition boxing has very nearly died out now, but it was very popular then and it was nothing for 20 or more to enter a novices comp.   I had already had a go at Bermondsey Baths, only to lose in the semi-finals to a boy called Rappaport who went on to win the final. I lost on a casting vote and because I was a Bermondsey boy the locals did not receive the verdict kindly.

When the chance came to try again I was keen to enter. I was just coming up to 18 and weighed around 11st 10lbs — it did not worry me in the slightest that the competition I had entered was for men up to 12st 7lbs.

The tournament was run by the Railway Police Club but was, in fact, an amateur night for the National Sporting Club who had then moved away from their old headquarters in Covent Garden. Like a lot of comps, so many people wanted to enter that first of all they drew names out of a hat just to see who was going to take part. I was lucky along with 15 others, which meant fighting four times in the one evening to win the Cup. The usual thing was for the promoting club to run a competition in a weight where they had a good boxer themselves, and they would put up the Cup. Well, this time the home boy did not win.

I had Tommy Till, who is dead now, in my corner, along with a chap we used to call 'Fat Charlie', Charlie Hardcastle. After I won my semi-final they had to take me out for a walk; I was desperate for air because with all the smoke in that hall I could hardly get my breath. I recovered all right for the final and went in with a fellow from the Belsize Club who bored in like a rugger player. All I could see was the top of his head so I just kept jabbing away at his forehead and won on points.

Then we came home on the bus, with Tommy and Charlie recalling the days when they would have taken a taxi home from the club in style and filled the Cup up with beer on the spot. I was not bothered about that, and could not afford it anyway, but I was walking on air all the same.

Back in Alscot Road brother Sid was standing on the pavement talking to a friend. 'How did you get on?' he asked. There was me with a big black eye and the Cup hidden under my coat. 'Oh, I got beat' I replied, and he was off, straight up to mum and dad who were in bed. 'He shouldn't box, dad' says Sid. 'Look at his face, he can't win nothing.' Mother sat up then. 'Look at him, Arthur. He shouldn't box.' Things had gone far enough so I pulled out the Cup, much to father's delight because he was a nut for any kind of sport. Next night it was all round to the pub to make sure that the trophy was christened properly. Just at that time I reckon even the family began to see me as a future world champion. Only things did not work out quite like that.

War was on the way. I cannot remember being particularly bothered about it even though I knew I would be among the first to go, along with many more of the Oxford and Bermondsey Club boys. Some time before, when it was planned to form a Militia, we all signed up with the Territorials and that meant just about the whole club. In fact I estimate that seventy-five per cent signed on, and after we had completed our first camp at Falmer near Brighton we were back home for only a fortnight before the ballon went up, as they said then, and we were off to be real soldiers.

When we signed on at the Queen's Drill Hall in Jamaica Road we were following in the footsteps of the club boys who had volunteered before the first 'do', and even more of them never came back. It may seem corny now, although it certainly does not to me, but the club motto was 'Fratres' which means brothers and we were taught a lot about club spirit. This was very strong indeed. We cared about it and that covered everyone, the footballers, the boxers, the lot. We were fit and very much together. The club members signed on *en masse* for the Great War and it simply seemed right for us to do the same for the next lot. We had no idea what we were in for, that our lives were going to be changed, our careers altered. Quite a few were lost but we Bermondsey boys went with the very best of intentions.

3

War-and a Long Road Home

Harry Gibbs's war started in a pub, a favourite local in Bermondsey where most of the club lads had gathered on the Friday before war was declared. With Mr Chamberlain demanding this, that and the other off Herr Hitler, and getting sod all, the Army sent for the Bermondsey Territorials. Down to Larby's they came to fetch us up to the Drill Hall. We finished off our pints and joined the colours. I was in the Queen's Royal Regiment, B Company, along with all the rest of the Stansfield Club boys. Funnily enough, I was the only boxer in that particular mob, but a lot of my mates, fellows I had grown up with, were on parade with me.

We went over to France on April Fool's Day 1940, and on 21 May I went into the bag, there to remain for five years. I am terrible at dates, but those two will be etched in my mind for ever.

When we landed in Cherbourg it was Shank's Pony all the way across France, finally ending up at a place near the Belgian border called Sternwerk. The Belgians welcomed us in like heroes when the Germans invaded and we were ready in the front line to face them, one of the first mobs into action.

We were dug in beside the Oudenarde Canal and for a bunch of kids very new indeed to military action it was a pretty frightening period. I remember our two captains well, Captain Lockwood who was the senior, and Captain Trench. Our orders were simple 'Last man, last round', and there we were stuck. One company, D company under Sgt-Major Brien, got away and I believe the idea was that eventually we would all retreat one behind the other. Some of our lot did get away to fight another action back near Sternwerk and eventually about 150 made it all the way home off the Dunkirk beaches.

I was not to share that little drama. I was in the platoon in reserve, No. 12 under Sgt-Major Burns, firmly dug in in the weapon pits and waiting for the Germans to make their move. Finally we were told that No. 10 and No. 11 platoons had been overrun in the woods in front of us and we were to surrender.

A lot of my memories are hazy because a great many things happened at once, but I'll never forget the scene as we came out with our hands up. We could see our other lads they had captured and there were thousands of Germans, and I do mean thousands. Bullets were still flying about and the lad who came out next to me copped one right through the head. One of our chaps stayed in the weapon pit, a bloke named Barrow. Maybe he wanted to be a hero, or perhaps he was too scared to come out, but whatever his reason for staying put he opened up with a brengun. A German officer was caught in the shoulder and there was chaos all round. It all quietened down in the end, and as we sorted ourselves out I found that one of my great mates, Georgie Tucker, was shot through the ankle. 'Don't leave me, Harry' he said, so I started to help him along.

As the Germans herded us back behind their advance we dropped further and further behind the main body until we came across a German artillery unit complete with an officer on a horse wearing a fine blue mac. For three days we had been without a drink because we were under fire and trapped, so I promptly asked him for water. To our relief he understood and passed me his water bottle. Big-hearted Harry passes it straight on to George who promptly drank every drop! Even now I have a go at him about that. Anyway, a couple of miles up the road we were separated and Georgie was dead worried because of all the stories we had heard about them shooting the wounded. He finished up all right though and I spotted him a couple of times after we arrived in the camps in Poland.

First things first though, and immediately after we were captured it was the Jerries' turn to give us some marching practice. They made us step it out as far as Brussels, and then loaded us on cattle trucks to our first camp at Bremen Würde Sandbostel. There they handed each of us a letter card to write home, and every last one of us asked for food to be sent out.

As the Germans sorted things out — and they must have found themselves with one hell of a lot of prisoners on their hands — they moved us on into Poland where we finished up in XXB at Marienberg, which was a French camp with British and Yugoslavs there as well.

For my part during the first year in captivity I really went through it from a health point of view. I grew more and more run down and was in and out of hospital several times. I had boils all over my neck and began to think I would never get rid of them. We used to wash in snow and the German soap they issued to us occasionally. They called it Rif and it was like sand. It stank the place out and I dread to think what was in it. Happily I was a very fit young man, though. I must have been because I pulled through and the next time I came under medical supervision I must confess it was self-imposed.

The Germans did their best to put us to work and our main objective in life was to avoid doing it. My mate Joe Bunce actually got a bloke to pour a saucepan of boiling water on to a sock placed over his arm. Only it did not scald him so he ran after the fellow and got him to do it all over again. This time it came up in a dirty great blister all over the arm. Really nasty! Our MO threatened that if anyone else came in with a self-inflicted injury he would have him on a charge. Joe had a terrible arm and I know he has the scars today because we have always kept in touch.

My game was to whack myself on the knee. I developed sinovitis of the knee and every time it came up I could not go to work. Dr Rose had me in hospital and shook his head: 'I can't understand it, Gibbs. Every time I get the damn thing better it comes back.' I told him it was standing about at all those roll calls, when the Germans had us waiting on our feet for hours. The doc tumbled me of course but he put me on sick picket which meant I carried a yellow card with an official German stamp on it. I showed it to Joe and he said he wasn't going to mess about with that. He found himself a Kraft Cheese packet which was the same kind of yellow as the official card, and then pinched a German stamp with the eagle on it.

That little racket did not last long, but Joe was always up to something and he was just one of the characters I met up with in the camps. I shall always remember one bloke, a bit of a nutter whose thing was writing long letters to Winston Churchill. Of course they never got out of camp, in fact they never even reached the Germans. Our fellows doing the censoring used to read them, have a good laugh and then put their heads together to work on a reply. When the fellow received it he would call us all round and read it out, firmly believing it was Winnie himself taking the trouble to tell him all about the war effort. You can imagine the kind of things he read out — 'Well, we chased those so-and-so Jerries out of Tobruk' or 'We sank another fifteen German battleships last week.'

If we had that chap on a string, Sammy McCarthy did the same to us for quite a while until we tumbled him. In our early days in the camps he made up his own news bulletins, but kidded us they were genuine. Although the Germans were on the prowl and what he was doing was forbidden, round he would come to each hut, announcing himself by beating a tin plate — 'boom-boom, boom-boom' just like the start of a proper broadcast. Then, sounding just like a newsreader, he would outline the news. On such-and-such a date the British Army had won this or that battle, the Germans were in full retreat, the RAF shooting the hell out of the Luftwaffe and the Navy was in charge of the Atlantic, the Pacific and every other ocean you care to name. Morale was sky high, of course, but then someone got hold of a real wireless and we realised that old Sammy was the biggest liar in the business, a con merchant in a pleasant way.

Spud Danford was another bloke who kept the old morale up with his monologues and, like Sammy, he was doubly welcome in those early months behind the wire. I will always remember one in particular which began 'It was Bethnal Green on a Saturday night, and another kid run over'. I was only nineteen-years-old and very impressionable. I must confess I was moist round the eyes as it took my mind back to Bermondsey and home, and after all Bethnal Green was only just across the river from us.

In all the time I was a prisoner I only boxed once, and that was at Marienberg when I fought a Scotsman called Cleets McKenzie with the distance agreed at three one-minute rounds. It may seem brief but I doubt if either of us had the strength to fight longer than two-minute rounds and it was only put on to cheer the lads up. In the end we still had to battle over four rounds. After three they said they could not separate us. There were a lot of Scots in the camp and all the judges were Scots who, doubtless, had all their fags wagered on their own man.

Cleets was out of the Seaforths, a hardened career soldier who had been a champion out in India. I was only a youngster compared to him, but I was faster on my feet and youth told in that final round. The Scots did not dare to give him the verdict and my mates collected the fags. A week later, I am sad to say, I was standing at old Cleets's funeral in the Marienberg cemetery. He came from the north and it seems he was a pretty dour sort of a bloke. He was out with a party chopping wood and when this German guard gave one lad a smack, Cleets muttered something like 'You German bastard'. Because he had an axe in his hand and seemed about to attack he was shot, anyway that was the German's story.

A great many of our adventures centred round the quest for food, and we had a few laughs as well. One of our blokes flogged his big old Army vest to a Pole in exchange for three loaves of bread, and when he brought them back to the Hell's Kitchen (that is what we called our hut) he showed no sign at all of share and share alike. There we all sat, gathered round like a pack of wolves, always bloody hungry and looking for any chance of an extra bite. The loaves were long and flat, typical Polish loaves, rye bread and black-looking stuff that must have been difficult to swallow after a while.

Finally he could force no more down and he took the one remaining loaf, put it under his head and used it as a pillow. During the night the lads cut the ends off as close as they could, leaving him asleep on about a quarter of the loaf. In the morning the bloke went rushing around wanting to cut the culprit's head off but no one was worried. The evidence had all been eaten within seconds.

Every prisoner dreams of freedom and when my chances to break out came along I took them all, even if there was not too much chance of making it home from prison camps inside Poland. This was particularly true during the winter months when it was difficult to think of anything except basic survival in some of the coldest weather I have known.

My mother sent out her first parcel, at least it was the first one to get through, and in it were two RAF-type shirts in speckled blue. Just what I needed for an escape outfit, and I was wearing one when I made my first bid. The other went to my partner on the run, Sonny Richards, who now lives in Northampton and remains a good friend of mine.

We were with a party sent out to live and work on a local farm — there were 30 or so Englishmen on farms in that particular area — and the first night there, out we went through the window. It was summer, still daylight and we should have had our heads examined going so early. As we clambered down there was a woman standing opposite. She looked Polish or even Russian and we told each other we were all right and she wouldn't say anything. How wrong can you be. Within seconds she had raised the alarm and their Dad's Army, Home Guard or fire watchers, whatever they called them, turned up in force.

The problem was that a lot of the Poles were helping the Germans. I do not blame them, they simply had to do it, but we could have done without that lady being right on the spot. The local lads were out on patrol already and when she started shouting over they came at the double. We were running for a cornfield not a hundred yards from the farm when they opened up on us, and down went Sonny.

Now I had a bad knee as I told you, but I was a long way in front going like Jesse Owens when the rifles opened up. As Sonny went over I debated whether to go back, decided to do the decent thing and went to see how he was.

'What's up Sonny? Have you been hit?' I asked. 'They're firing at us' he replied.

'I know that you silly bastard,' I said, 'get up and run for your life.'

We made it to the cornfield and as we ran through it we threw off our gear, haversacks, anything to lighten the load. After the corn came a stream and if it had been twenty feet deep we would still have run through the bottom with fear. Up the far bank we shot and on into another farm-yard. There we hid in a barn, up on the top of the hay, and our hiding place did not fool our pursuers in the slightest. In came the farmer and left his two Alsatians below us and closed the barn door. That was the end of the escape and we were still perched on the stack when the militia lads came rushing in.

It is easy to write that we were sentenced to twenty-one days, and then pass on, but I can tell you that those three weeks meant an extremely unpleasant time for the many prisoners who were forced to face up to it – and did so time and again rather than knuckle down and stop causing the Germans bother.

The worst thing about the punishment cells was the boredom. After two or three days you didn't have any more sleep left in you, you had no books and no games to pass the time. We used to shout to one another between the cells, but it was hardly a good way to carry on a conversation. Still, even bad times come to an end, and then it was back to the usual routine and more scheming for the next breakout.

My second try did not come for quite a while, and then the chance came out of the blue after I received a parcel sent out by the Variety Club of Great Britain. Inside were two pairs of socks and a ringboard game. 'They must think we're mental out here sending kids games', I thought, but we still stuck it up on the back of the hut door and started to throw the rubber rings at the hooks on the board.

As I went up to collect the rings after my first throw I noticed the trademark on the board, ZEBO, and that started bells ringing inside my brain. Down came the board and I was off, round to see the doctor and the padre who were key men in the escape committee. You see ZEBO was the codeword we had been ordered to look out for, and when we opened up the back of that board we found all sorts of things packed inside. There were dyes, maps of Stetin docks and a variety of other information to assist escapers. The board was sent out to me and I was given the chance to test the information it contained.

This time the escape was carefully planned, and I was to make for Gdynia, or Gottenharven as we called it then. I was ordered to memorise the name of a café — the Café Grubenau — where I was to make contact with Swedish sailors. They ferried coal across the Baltic and some were prepared to take stowaway escapers back to neutral Sweden. My partner for the trip was a Scotsman called Alex Duncan, yet another ex-prisoner with whom I have kept in touch over the years, and although we failed in the end we were out for more than two weeks after legging it away from one of the farms.

Needless to say I didn't set off in broad daylight this time and we slipped clear without trouble. There were locks on the windows and doors where we were locked up but the screws were all loose — the lads had it all sorted out. Each evening we looked for a farm where some of our lads were working and instead of breaking out we broke in. We slept under the bunks and hid there when the guards came in. In the mornings the lads were unlocked, and when they went off to work we slipped away again, and the Jerries never knew we had been there.

Finally we reached the River Vistula, and found it was much too wide to get across. We hunted around and eventually came to a bridge at Dirshau, but crossing it remained an almighty problem. The Germans were having plenty of trouble with the partisans (those Poles like a fight, you know) and they were guarding the bridge in strength.

Not far down the river a group of children were fishing and to our delight we spotted that they had a boat with them. We were wearing baggy brown outfits, made out of prison blankets, with a letter P on them to signify that we were Poles. So we were not too dismayed when the kids turned out to be Germans who spoke only a little Polish, like us. We put over the message that we wanted to be rowed to the other side. They asked why and we mentioned going to a party. They swallowed our story and that was one more hurdle crossed.

Once over the Vistula we made progress until we had

about thirty kilometres left to go to the coast. As we went into a small village we pulled up a couple of Polish girls and tried to ask them if there were any British prisoners in the village or working in the district. They could not understand us, but a fellow came along with a smattering of English and said there were a few just through the village.

By this time it was close to curfew and as we went down the village street the burgomaster, mayor or whatever they called him, was waiting with his rifle, a sort of shotgun actually. We'll never know if he was tipped off, but he looked as if he meant business so we went quietly. Into the local cobbler's shop he marched us, and then punched Alex because he thought he was a Pole. Then he spotted some Canadian chocolate that we'd been given at the last place we holed up, and he realised who he had captured.

We spent the evening in the cellar and an old lady served us up these beautiful potatoes in their jackets in exchange for the chocolate. All round we were reasonably comfortable, apart from being bagged again, until the middle of the night when they sent two soldiers from the battalion guarding the bridge round to collect us. One had a bike and the pair of them soon had us out on the march all the way back to the railway station at Elbin. I shall remember that march for ever. I was wearing a pair of German jackboots and the blisters on both feet grew worse and worse until I was in terrible pain.

'Look' I whispered to Alex Duncan, 'you take one, I'll finish the other, and we're away again.' He nearly had a fit. 'Don't do it Harry' he urged, 'or we'll both be shot.' Anyway I let him talk me out of it, and I limped into the station. As we sat there getting our breath back, the Poles were streaming past on their way to work and the girls were pointing us out as Fluchtlingers, which means runaways.

Back in camp Alex was lucky. He was given seven days while I had the full twenty-one because I had hoofed it off before. Funnily enough, some time after I was home some

Government department or other got in touch and after I had filled in a whole lot of forms they sent me £62 to cover loss of equipment while escaping. At least I think that is what it was all about, and I was pleased anyway because it was a lot of money then.

Just once more I went on the run, but by then we were out of the camps and the situation was chaotic as the Germans cleared out in the face of the Russian advance. We were on the road for two days before a group of us simply walked off to see if we could fend a bit better for ourselves. By this stage the guards were not too vigilant and a number of them even slipped away with some of the lads.

One of the blokes with me was Georgie Merritt who was a footballer and whose cousin was a pro boxer. I think Georgie was with Arsenal and Margate, which was like a nursery club, and then went to Derby County just before the war. He was still with me, and so was my old escape comrade Sonny Richards, when the Wehrmacht, doing a sweeping up job, rounded up about thirty of us. This time we were stuck in a proper prison, a Polish one with wire netting slung over the balconies to stop anyone slinging himself off. It was so near the fighting we could hear the Russian guns and on the ground floor the place was packed with Russians, many of them not long captured.

Then the Germans marched in about 500 Jewesses from Lithuania, and if we were not already well aware what the war was all about we were left under no illusions. You could barely recognise those kids as women, and many of them were suffering terribly from gangrene caused by frost-bite.

It was lucky for the British lads that we were there only two or three days because those Russians would have made sure we were slaughtered if their troops had arrived in time to take us. The Germans put the British in charge of the rations and we made sure the women had all the food, which was not so much in any case, while the Russians went without.

Just ahead of the Red Army advance we were loaded onto a train packed with wounded German soldiers and we found ourselves on a real Cook's tour back into Germany. We went round the back of Stetin, to Berlin and at camp after camp we were turned away. After all those years of trying to get out of a camp, now we were trying to get in. All of them were full and refused to take us. In the end we wound up all the way back at Sandbostel, the first camp we were taken to when we were captured at Oudenarde.

The camp was full of Russians and soon after our arrival they marched in a long file of political prisoners, the ones with the pyjama jackets on, yes just like those some of you may have seen in those dreadful pictures from Belsen or Dachau. You could not really say those poor fellows marched, though, because of the state they were in. They dragged themselves past us and you've never seen anything like it, and nor do you ever want to. We said to each other 'People simply won't believe it'. Well I saw it, I actually did and I'll never forget it.

The next day we were on our way once more because typhoid broke out and we were taken to Milag about sixteen kilometres away. This time we found ourselves in what had been a naval camp. They put us in the merchant seamen's section but the place was already full of Americans who had been captured in the Ardennes. Dysentery was rampant at Milag and those poor Yanks were dying like flies.

So far as camps went this was journey's end, and all that remained was a grandstand view of the battle before we were liberated. The Americans said Paton would be coming through but it was the good old Guards Armoured who arrived on the scene first. It was amazing: they fought their way round the camp with us in the middle watching like a crowd at a football match. The tracer was zipping across, the tanks were rolling — I am sorry to say that we saw six or seven of our own knocked out — and finally it was over, the gates were open and we were free at last.

After that things moved fast and I must say they wasted no time in getting us home. One night in Brussels, and there the Salvation Army took charge. They did a marvellous job and were the first people we saw from outside the military world. That may well be the reason I never say no when their collecting box comes round. One of the Sally Army girls handed out a bar of soap, a face flannel and a packet of Woodbines. Being prisoners of war we all went round twice.

Next morning we were flown home. It was nothing grand in the way of a plane, but I've never enjoyed a flight so much. I've travelled first class across the world on Jumbo jets but it could never beat that hop home from Belgium. We landed two or three days before VE Day and as we climbed out of the plane at an airstrip near Tring the WAAV girls were waiting for us. Nothing romantic mind, just 'Step this way into this hangar, lads,' and a quick spray of DDT or something like that.

Next they showed us this big room with a wonderful spread all laid out, but then came the let-down. 'Naval and RAF personnel this way' they said, 'Army personnel this way.' In went the Navy and RAF lads to tuck in while we were ushered straight out to lorries. What a disappointment and then, just to rub it in, the driver lost his way and took hours getting us to a camp near Amersham. We were given a fiver each and were told that the doctor would be round to check us over in the morning. We would be ready to set off for home by midday. That old doctor had an easy job: by morning most of the lads, and the Londoners in particular, had jumped the wire. No guns to stop us this time.

Back in Alscot Road I headed for number 50, remember

number 20 was bombed, and down I went into the basement. Dad was standing there in his braces shaving in the mirror on the wall. I tapped him on the shoulder and when he turned round he literally staggered against the wall with shock.

I must say I have often felt guilty about giving him such a jolt. The Army had sent a telegram from Brussels to say I was out and on the way, and I never intended to upset him. It even crossed my mind later that a shock like that might have brought on the cancer that killed him within the year, but I must say he rapidly recovered that day and soon summoned up a family shindig.

Brother Sid, a staff sergeant by this time, was just back from Norway and stationed in Wales. He was able to get leave, and my eldest brother, stationed at Chatham with the Navy, raced for home as well. Two days later I went back to Amersham to hear all the lads talking about the great time they had had and how everyone bought them loads of drink.

Then at last it hit me that I was home. My lot gave me a great welcome, although it was me who bought the booze while they sat back and sank it. The fiver went and another tenner beside, but what the hell — it was great to be home.

4

A Girl With My Tea

Back to routine Army life, and back to boxing — that was the order of the day until it was time for demob. I was promoted to Corporal PTI, stationed at Shirley near Croydon and most days I took my lads down to Mitcham Barracks for training. Naturally I was longing for the day when I would have my first proper contest since before the war, but as it turned out the first fight I had was what might be described as an extra-curricular activity. It nearly put me on a charge, but in fact I won not only the fight but in the end a far, far greater prize — my wife Phyllis.

Down at Mitcham we were regular visitors to the NAAFI queue. Virtually the lot of us were ex prisoners-of-war and we were always hungry. On this particular day we were having some backchat with a crowd of ATS girls and I set out to make an impression by offering to pay for all the teas. At 2d a cup I felt a real tycoon. But this girl who I had never seen before, brought me back to earth with a bump: 'Great stuff, soldier' she said, 'we get more money than you do anyway.' When we got talking she asked me where I came from. 'Kensington' I said, still trying to lay it on a bit. 'More like the Old Kent Road' came back the sharp reply, and she wasn't far out either was she?

It all started from that early bit of verbal sparring and we saw each other pretty often as she was on the lorry that brought up the rations to Shirley. Along with the lorry came the opposition; the driver was a big ginger-headed corporal who was also after her affections — playing Bluto to my Popeye! He was jealous of me, I was jealous of him and the situation simply had to boil up before very long.

The crunch came the day I had a warning word with him for lifting her down off the tailboard of the lorry by the hips. 'Don't do that, old chap' I said, or something like that anyway.

It did not make for a good atmosphere when I jumped up on the lorry for a lift back to Mitcham. I had with me my leather case full of boxing gear and when he dropped Phyl by the ration store I stood talking to her with my case just in the road. He deliberately reversed the lorry over the case which busted wide open and all my gear was crushed.

Just to add to my displeasure Phyl ran off laughing and that really stirred me up. Round to the garage I went to find his lordship busy telling the story to a crowd of mechanics. I shoved the remains of the case into his hand and ordered: 'Right, round to the CO, he can sort this out.' As we marched towards the headquarters office the bloke on the gate, an ex POW who knew me, said, 'What's up, Harry?' When I told him he replied that I knew the best thing to do.

So, without more ado, right outside the office, I chinned the fellow. The RSM saw it, in fact just about everyone saw it and we were whipped in front of Major Rimmington, another former prisoner-of-war. The story was told and it turned out that this bloke, who was a lot bigger than me — and I'm not small — was the bully of the barracks and they had been looking for a way to shift him out. This was it. Rimmington told him he was a big coward and that he would have to pay for a new case and next day he was posted on his way. The same evening I wanted Phyl to sit next to me in the canteen but she refused because it was all round the camp that two corporals were fighting over her.

I never faced a charge over the punch-up and the next year, 1946, Phyllis and I were married. We took the plunge on £122 — her gratuity and mine — and started off living with Phyl's mother in Turnpike Lane, Wood Green. Her family originally came from Islington but shifted to Wood Green when they were bombed out. We never lived in Bermondsey, in fact I have not lived there since. I kept my Bermondsey connections, of course, and went round to Mum's for midday dinner most days, just like my other brothers. Eventually Phyl and I moved off to Seven Kings where I owned my first house, and then to Brentwood where I now have a cosy little home. My daughter Sheila, our only child, lives just down the road with our grandchildren Nicola and Matthew, a lively pair who give us a vast amount of pleasure.

The first contest I had with the gloves on after the war would have cost me my amateur status well ahead of time if the Amateur Boxing Association, still the most rigid of bodies, had found out. I was talked into having a go in the boxing booth at a fair in Croydon. A whole crowd of lads who were stationed at Shirley went down and I joined the gathering throng outside Wood's Boxing Booth. It was the old-style booth with the fighters lined up outside looking for challenges from the crowd — a sight that has almost gone these days as the booths are dying out. In the end I shouted up and went behind the scenes to be kitted out.

They lent me a pair of boots and put me in with a fellow named Johnny Cunningham, an old pro from Bethnal Green who was a lot older than me and had finished his career. The advertised prizes at stake were £2 if you went the distance and £8 if you stopped the bloke or knocked him out. As it turned out all I got was ten bob, even though I went the distance. All through, Cunningham was talking in my ear: 'Steady up son, steady up, take it easy', and then I was handed a ten bob note and had to be satisfied. It was only a bit of fun but it would have turned me pro if the amateur officials had found out.

After that I went back to the Oxford and Bermondsey Club to pick up my own career properly. The promising lad who went off to war had lost more than five years boxing time, and I never did make it up which was not surprising after all that time in the camps. Of course it affected me, particularly when eventually I tried my luck as a professional. I was fine and fast over six rounds but all boxers, no matter how fast they are, come under increasing pressure the more tired they become, say over ten rounds. Much as I loved competitive boxing I would have been hard pushed to do ten rounds.

It took a long time to recover when I came home, although we were the lucky ones because we did come back. So many lads went to Burma and places like that and did not come home, or if they did they had suffered far more than I did. But when I fought again something had been taken away, although it is hard to know exactly what it was, perhaps just that vital edge in stamina. Mind you it never took my sense of humour away, in fact it probably added to it.

At first the Army gave me a pension because of the bad knee I developed in Marienburg, but after only about three months they changed their minds and bought me out of it. They put me on the scales, checked the knee over and sent me £28 to clear the matter up. They knew I was back boxing and I could hardly take a disability pension.

I soon became a regular performer on the amateur shows that started up as the war ended, although once again I was very nearly turned pro before my time when it was stated that H. Gibbs of Bermondsey had entered a competition for professional heavyweights at Watford. Boxing News of 21 November 1945 carried a disclaimer that L/Cpl. H. Gibbs (Oxford and Bermondsey B.C.) was not the H. Gibbs mentioned, was an amateur and planning to stay that way. Of course, it was me down on the list at Watford, but some of my mates had put me in. I never was a heavyweight and certainly was not ready to turn pro at that stage.

At Bermondsey Baths I boxed a docker called Paddy Griffin and lost on a casting vote, but I was still picked to represent London soon afterwards as a light-heavyweight. The match was at the Seymour Hall, against Wales I think, and I won on points. After that I remember losing to a bloke named Street on a disqualification at Beckenham Baths and then gaining my revenge over Griffin.

When it came to the South East London divisional championships — the first step on the way to an ABA title — I lost in the final to a fellow called Gall, who eventually moved off to Australia. That year he went right through to the national finals where he finished as runner-up. Gall belonged to the famous Lynn Athletic Club from Walworth who were trained by old Matt Wells, a great character who had been an amateur and pro champion and really knew the game — and I reckon it was Matt who beat me. Before the final Griffin came into the dressing room to wish me luck. He had beaten Gall and reckoned I would win the title. As it turned out I was over-confident; I lifted my chin and he caught me right on the adam's apple. It put me right off and I was stopped. Old Matt knew I could jab a bit as well as punch and sent the fellow out to get stuck in. He did and it paid off, although I beat him in a return at Manor Place Baths.

But my big moment as an amateur was yet to come. Nowadays I remember the occasion vividly, although my opponent that momentous night tells me he does not recall it at all. In 1946 or '47 I was matched with Don Scott, who went on to win a Silver medal when the Olympic Games were held in London in 1948. We met at the Croydon Civic Hall and Don was a very strong favourite. He was in the Guards at the time, a red-cap I believe, and even had Guards officers there to watch him that night. Old Dan Titchener opted out of my corner. 'Sorry son' he said, 'I'm not coming in the corner because you've got no chance.' My brother-in-law Johnny Allen was not so pessimistic: 'Right, I'll help you Harry' he said.

The first round was not so good from my angle. I could not get out of the way of his educated left hand, but Johnny had an answer. 'Now look Harry,' he whispered in my ear, 'as he goes to lead that jab you throw your right over the top of his left.' Never has corner advice worked better — in fact Don jabbed, I hurled over the right and it caught him flush on the side of the jaw. He went out like a light.

Years later I bumped into Don at a Boxing Writers' Club dinner — always the best gathering of any year for boxing people — and he said to me: 'Harry, you say you boxed me once but you know I can't remember it.' I know I hit him hard, but not that hard! 'Sorry Donald' I replied, 'If you look at the records you'll see I knocked you out. It was just one of those things. I don't like to think that Johnny Prince stopped me when I was a professional, but he did.'

Finally, like so many amateurs, I decided the time had arrived to try my luck as a pro and I applied for a licence. I was surrounded by friends: Billy Cottrell was my manager, Danny Holland was trainer while Danny Mahoney helped out in the corner. And never let anyone talk to me about fighters being exploited. I'm not saying it never happens of course, but not one of those blokes ever took a penny off me.

My career was moderately successful, but brief. It covered only seven fights and I won the first six, starting on home ground at Bermondsey Baths against a fellow called Williams. I came straight from work in the docks to the hall, wearing my old mac which was going to double up as my dressing gown in the ring. They were billing Williams as Freddie Mills's sparring partner and there he was done up like a dog's dinner, real smart with a proper boxing gown and everything.

George Daly was top of the bill, and he came across to

have a word. 'Don't worry Harry' he told me, 'you'll not only beat him you'll stop him' And I did. It was the first of three appearances as a pro in Bermondsey. All my mates came off the wharf to have a laugh and see me take a hiding, but I'm delighted to say I never did — not there anyway.

The Cottrells promoted that first show I fought on and I earned £6 for six rounds, although it did not go the distance. Another time we all went off to Maidstone on a terrible foggy evening. My bloke turned up and I knocked him out, but the show was running so short that Billy agreed to strip off and boxed an exhibition with Randolph Turpin, then one of the great prospects in British boxing.

Six fights, six wins, but Harry Gibbs called a halt. I was working in the docks and realised even then that I would never have the stamina to reach the top, however hard I trained. I fought only once more, and that was to do a favour. Billy or Danny Holland, I forget which, rang me at Turnpike Lane. Promoter Harry Droy was stuck, would I fight Johnny Prince at the Caledonian Baths in Islington. I had not been in training, but I called up to Phyllis, who was pregnant at the time: 'I'm just going down to the Caledonian Baths to get a couple of wheels for the baby's pram.' She tried to talk me out of it but I had decided to have just one more go.

In the first round I jabbed his head off, but by the second or third — not long anyhow — I was out of gas. I went down and, somehow, misjudged the count, not by a lot but just enough. As the referee Benny Caplan said 'Nine and out' I was just starting up. As he called 'out' I showed out about it. Caplan, later my partner as a pro referee on many occasions, came upstairs afterwards. 'Don't show me up like that, son' he said. 'What?' I replied, 'You showed me up. I'd been training specially for that fight and you do that to me.' Danny and Billy did not know how to keep a straight face. All I can say after all this time is 'Sorry, Ben.'

I earned £6 10s for the fight and as we were leaving the dressing room the ring whip asked for money. 'Leave it out' said Dan. 'You get nothing off this kid. He only got £6 10s.'

So a career ended, but as one door closes another one opens. Not always true I suppose, but it was for me because soon afterwards I answered an advert for an instructor and started one of the happiest spells in all my years in boxing.

5

My Corinthians

When I spotted the advert for an instructor at the Belsize Boxing Club, I stepped into what was for me another world. I learned just what a great sport boxing is for its own sake and not just for its financial return, and that there really are some true Corinthians left in the world.

I made my way to Lloyds Bank in Lombard Street to be interviewed by the then secretary of the club, the late Bill Hastings. As true blue an amateur as you could meet anywhere, he still looked very much a boxer, complete with bent nose. It seems that in the days when amateurs and professionals sparred together regularly, he not only went into the ring with the great Ted Kid Lewis but even had the temerity to deal Ted a few shrewd blows that hurt him. Ted went to town and Hastings carried the signs for the rest of his life, at least that is the story.

Anyway, I was offered the job at 25 bob a night and a free supper. I was on four weeks probation and reported for duty on the first possible night at the club's headquarters at the London Scottish Drill Hall in Buckingham Gate. The club captain at the time was the remarkable Dick Calver who reigned for 15 years and is now the Belsize president, but after four weeks I told him: 'Well, that's it. Cheerio.' 'What are you talking about Gibbs' he said (they always called the instructors by their surnames, very much the old public school approach). 'I'm finishing because I was on a four-week trial and I've not heard from Mr Hastings' I replied. 'Oh no' said Calver, 'we're not letting you go, you must come back next week.' I did, never regretted it for a second and was with the club for fourteen years.

When I left the club to concentrate on my refereeing career I was presented with a silver salver which carries the words: 'To Harry Gibbs in grateful appreciation of his services to Belsize Boxing Club 1947 to 1961.' Along with the salver went a Belsize tie which was a great honour. The salver I will always treasure, but the right to wear the tie pleased me even more and I always wear it proudly at the club's Christmas supper.

Without a doubt my Belsize days were my happiest in boxing. I called the lads my Corinthians, and by golly they were just that: they would go anywhere to box for the fun of it. They were not bothered about prizes and they never claimed expenses. They boxed the Universities and Sandhurst, but were just as eager to box on open shows and in their time produced a healthy list of ABA champions.

Belsize is the oldest club in the country, despite clubs like Guys Hospital trying to claim the distinction, and was first formed to fight off footpads on Belsize Common and escort young ladies across in safety. For many years the club was exclusively for serving officers and public school boys, but when I was there they opened the gates to a wide range of blokes and the only requirement was that they shared the ideas on the sport that have always marked the Belsize.

Certainly it was a novel atmosphere for me, but I revelled in it. I am proud to have followed in the footsteps, or perhaps I should say glove marks, of many famous instructors, including Joe Bowker who figures in the famous boxing print 'A night at the National Sporting Club' in which he is shown in the ring with 'Peerless' Jim Driscoll. It is a picture I know well because it hangs in the boardroom of the British Boxing Board of Control where I sit from time to time as a member of the referees' committee.

When first I joined Belsize the resident instructors were Tommy Slater, an old professional who was ABA lightweight champion in 1926, and Bill Williams, at that time himself a 'Star' class pro referee and also well-known as boxing instructor at St Paul's School.

My way of instructing was to spar with my boxers at every training session and this sometimes got me into some odd situations, and none stranger than with Dr Pat Leahy, a former Irish champion who was later a well-known figure in Harley Street. The doctor had lost a leg in the war but he still liked to keep in training. We regularly sparred a round or two and false leg or not he dug out some useful punches.

Belsize brought out a book about the club and its history and I was honoured to be mentioned here and there. I am sure they will not mind my repeating one or two extracts about my period with them:

'Once, when we had boxed Trinity College in Dublin, we had a nightmare journey back by air with delays all night and a variety of excuses proferred. We reached London in the early morning tired and dispirited, and some of us worried whether we could get to work on time, and were bundled into a bus. It stood there in silence for several minutes to our exasperation, until Harry's voice was heard 'What's holding us up now — it can't be headwinds.'

'He was a wonderful man in the corner and must have won many a contest for the club in that capacity. I remember once, when Peter Tunnell was having a particularly frustrating and busy contest at Oxford and came back to his corner at the end of the second round, very crestfallen and wagging his head in despair. No one knows what Harry said in the interval, and it may not have been polite, but Peter shot off his stool and so belaboured his opponent the decision was never in doubt from then on.'

Many of my Belsize men were real characters. George Wright, who died in Australia not long back, certainly was, and so was 'Butch' McKenzie-Hill. I seconded him when he met Johnny Ould at the Royal Albert Hall and he crowned his career by boxing for England against Russia.

He reached the top class despite the restricted use of one arm which was because of an injury received on active service, I believe.

Two of my lads, Paul Gormley and Johnny Simmonds, turned pro, which was rare indeed for Belsize members, and Terry Hollis, a particular protégé of mine, boxed for Great Britain. I trained Terry at the Stock Exchange Club, too, and he started his working life as a Blue Button Boy in the Exchange. Now he is a stock broker in his own right.

I have no doubt at all that my association with Belsize has had a great effect on my career as a referee, in fact on my life as a whole. Working with these boys gave me a wonderful insight into the way boxing really is a sport of distinction, however much people may try to discredit it. Much the same could be said, too, of the Stock Exchange Club. When I was training them we used the floor of the Exchange itself when the day's business was over, and we put up as many as four rings at a time the interest was so great. The Blue Button Boys boxed and so did some of the jobbers. After my time one of the Blue Button lads, Mickey Carter, won an ABA title and went on to box in the Olympic Games, although not as a Stock Exchange member!

The Belsize Club used to support the Sea Cadets at Stoke Newington and in the days when the Sea Cadets National Championship was a big thing in youth boxing I used to train them as well. And while I was helping the cadets one of their captains was involved with St Pancras who needed an instructor. They snapped me up and then I was so busy I must have seemed like a stranger to Phyllis, I was out so much.

St Pancras was loaded with useful boxers and I shared the training duties with Freddie Webster. Freddie was a fine operator but much older than me which meant that I did all the work in the ring with the lads. When Fred retired I said I would stay on provided they paid the tax for me on the wages they gave me. They refused and so we had to part.

As my adventures with these famous clubs progressed I found myself gaining recognition, first with London teams and then with the England national team. I was a paid instructor and one of the first professionals to take a national amateur team abroad — but things were easier between amateur and professional bodies than they are now. The ABA not only allowed me to do the job, they paid me as well.

For London my first trip as trainer was to Dublin and after that to Holland. I went with England to Frankfurt, and a team loaded with future professional champions, and finally to Italy on a two-match England tour in 1953 that proved extremely hectic and controversial.

In Germany the England team included five men later to win British titles as professionals, with two of them fighting for world championships. Dave Charnley and Henry Cooper were the pair, and the others to win titles later were flyweight Frankie Jones, middle Ron Barton and heavyweight Joe Erskine. I have no particular memories of Cooper as an amateur, except that he was useful of course. I believe both he and Erskine lost on this expedition, Charnley won and Barton got a draw which you can have in amateur boxing on the Continent. Famous amateurs on the trip who never became professionals were Gerald John and Bruce Wells. A picture of the team can be found in this book — it is very much one of my prized possessions.

In Italy all the fuss centred round Corporal Brian Harper of the RAF, a burly customer given to fixing opponents with a ferocious glare before swinging into action. The name may not mean a lot to you until I say that Harper was the family name, but his boxing name was London. Yes, Brian London, later to become British heavyweight champion and fight for the world title on two occasions, against Floyd Patterson and Muhammad Ali.

First stop was Milan where England met Italy at the National Theatre. In the ring the stools were placed not in opposite corners as is usual but in corners on the same side of the ring. It seems strange to us but the same arrangement was used not so long ago when Britain's Kevin Finnegan lost his European middleweight title to Italy's Matteo Salvemini in San Remo.

Harper was fighting a bulky Italian called Giovachino Bozzano with a Frenchman named Robert Vaisberg in charge. Monsieur Vaisberg, like many Continental referees, operated for both pro and amateur codes and had controlled Randolph Turpin's European title fight with Tiberio Mitri. He may have been experienced but I did not think he covered himself in glory in Milan.

He called Brian and Nino up to shake hands and under the amateur rules you then come out fighting. When Brian came back to the corner he checked with me: 'I don't shake hands again do I Harry?' I assured him he did not. The bell started round one and the Italian came out sticking his glove forward to shake hands. Brian promptly, and rightly, chinned him. The Italian crowd went mad with rage, and those Italians are an inflammable lot, while Bozzano draped himself all over Harper and hung on something awful. At the end of the round I told him 'Don't worry, son, you'll beat him.'

Misplaced confidence as it turned out. In the next round the referee alleged that Brian had butted the fellow and stuck his thumb in his eye. I would not have it and jumped up to protest. No disqualification but going into the third I told Brian: 'You won't get the decision here so you must stop him. You know the rules, at the bell go straight out.'

He obeyed orders to the letter, in fact almost too literally. The Italian second was slow to move out of the ring so Brian pulled him out of the way and thumped Nino while he was still on his stool. More crowd eruption, and Vaisberg seemed inclined yet again to disqualify my man. Naturally I protested and when it was over the crowd were shouting for blood and it was clear there was going to be trouble. The ring was up on the stage and the irate fans soon had us trapped. Luckily the caribinieri were out in force to protect us on our way out of the ring and down the stairs towards the dressing room.

As we went down I was protecting Brian as much as I could, taking a fair number of kicks along the way. Then I was shut out of the dressing room by mistake, and later on shoved up against the side of the charabanc. Anxious moments, but the police rescued me and finally the coach drove off with Brian hidden by my side along the back seat. The team manager, Christmas his name was, went off alarmingly at Brian, who told him his dad — Jack London the old British heavyweight champion — always told him that winners can laugh and losers can do what they like. Next stop was Perugia where Harper won comfortably. However, when we got home the ABA wanted to ban him, although he did box once more as an amateur. When Brian applied to turn pro the Board of Control asked me if I would recommend him. I said that I most definitely would because I felt he was the victim of thoroughly bad refereeing. He was a good performer but probably better as a pro than in his amateur days.

The trip to Italy turned out to be my last with England because the feeling against the pros hardened in the amateur ranks, which was disappointing for me and a great pity all round. So many people in amateur boxing clubs regard boxing as one sport. They are proud when their boxers go on to become pro champions and I am just as proud to have kept the friendship of so many of them. But there are those, in the higher echelons it seems to me, who are jealous because the amateur ranks are the nursery for the pro game, and you cannot alter that.

My own feeling is that if the amateurs employed more professional coaches even now they would do better in world boxing. The Belsize always employed professional instructors and enjoyed a happy relationship with them. The attitude that once a man is professional he is an outcast is very wrong. Most professionals have real dignity and many give up their time to help the amateurs — particularly the star pro boxers who are always turning out to back amateur events. I am a professional referee but I go all over the show for the amateurs, giving prizes away and helping them raise money. I do not do it for professional boxing but for the sport itself.

On one occasion I went to help get the collection going at a show in aid of some clerks injured in the docks. Well, amateurs do not even allow pros into the ring for guest appearances but on this occasion Bill Cox, who was ABA secretary at the time, said, 'Get in the ring, Harry. We don't regard you as a pro.' Fine, in I went to do the job, but the same courtesy should always be extended to Maurice Hope, Jim Watt, Alan Minter or any of the lads giving their services to help out. There is nothing dirty about being a pro and in so many sports the word has been abolished. That cannot happen in boxing, but I do wish the two sides were closer.

My move into pro refereeing, which came some time before I finally gave up as an amateur instructor, was sparked off by little Charlie Darby, one of the boxing writers who specialised in the amateur side of the sport. It happened when I was training a representative squad at the Railways Gym in Euston. Club trainers would bring their boxers up to me, and one Sunday morning Charlie was there when a bloke from the Polytechnic brought their heavyweight Dave Thomas over.

Dave, who died recently while out on a jogging run, was one of our best amateur heavyweights who never turned pro. He beat Billy Walker a couple of times and reached a

European Championship final. On this occasion he had arrived late, the others had gone or finished training and when the fellow with him asked who would spar I said I would. While we were getting ready it was whispered that Thomas's companion was saying I would not be much use as a sparring partner as I was too old. Well, as you can imagine I was none too pleased.

In the first round the kid jabbed my ears off and between rounds I said to Charlie, 'He's taking a few liberties here.' After that I pulled the boy close and gave him a first hand demonstration of a few tricks I had picked up on my travels. Afterwards the Poly fellow told me they were a bit uncalled for. 'Well,' I replied, 'so were your remarks about me being too old.'

When we got out Charlie had a go at me too. 'You can't keep up sparring with them all for ever' he warned me, 'something has to give sometime. Why don't you take up refereeing?' I told him I didn't see how I could, and in any case they probably didn't need any more. 'Strange you should say that' Charlie hit back, 'but the Boxing Board are setting up a course for new referees and they've announced it in Boxing News.'

I was well aware that Charlie was on the mark about the sparring, but I was just as certain that that was my way of training and I was not at all sure I wanted to carry on without being in there with the lads. So the seeds were sown, and they had to take root rapidly or the chance was lost. The answer to the dilemma you know already, and off I went into the unknown again to a future where the world opened up for me in a way I had never imagined in my wildest dreams.

6

'Old Toffee' in Charge

A life of continual interest, hard work and humour, touched occasionally by adventure and even danger, awaited me from 1946 onwards when my father died and I took over his dock registration. Of course, in no way was I stepping into the unknown because my family had connections with the docks which went back generations. The docks were a family business for the Gibbs clan. My father came from Custom House, which is close to the Albert Dock, and he belonged to a huge family with a load of brothers to say nothing of uncles and cousins. I believe the Gibbs hold the record for actually putting out a complete ship's gang from one family. It included the clerk and the crane driver, all members of the Gibbs family, and consisted of eleven in the gang with the other two making thirteen.

After being brought up with dock life I feel at home there and I reckon the dock workers are great people. It would be easy to write that, wouldn't it, but I know thousands of dockers and they know how I feel about them. I have my rows, lots of rows — and when you have a barney in the docks it is liable to be a humdinger. In my day I've thrown the odd punch or two to ram home a point, but I do not think I am regarded as a bully. In fact you could not be a bully and survive very long in any sort of position of authority in the docks. The lads know my views veer a bit towards the right. They give me the 'Land of Hope and Glory' bit, and these days the Maggie Thatchers as well, but they have always worked with me and for me, and given me that special companionship you find up and down the river bank.

When I took over from my father it was simply as a docker, although before long I became a ship worker or foreman. Just after the war I was working in the Tooley Street sector, No. 6 sector, and was operating at New Fresh Wharf as what they called a preference man. This meant that when there was a ship in I would receive first preference for getting a job ahead of outsiders, or men we called 'shapers' for a job.

Confusing? Well I suppose it is, but of course we lived with the system all the time. Shapers were men who had dockers' briefs — were registered that is — but did not go to any particular wharf regularly. If a man was shaping for work he had to be on the callstand by 7.45 am and if the foreman looking for men did not need him he went to report to Control. From Control he could be sent on to any other part of the docks where there was work available. So if he missed out at New Fresh Wharf he might end up at the Surrey Dock or the Albert.

I stayed on at New Fresh Wharf until about 1953 when, through my boxing connections, I found myself with a better job. I was training the Stock Exchange Club and helping the Insurance Boxing Club as well. There I met a gentleman named Geoff Double who was a top man of some sort in the Royal Insurance and part of his work was to insure wharfs owned by the Transport Development Group, or Spurlings as they were then called. He was a great friend of a Mr Fraser who was a top johnny in the group and when a job came up at Aberdeen Wharf in the London Docks he insisted that I leave Tooley Street and apply for the place.

After some thought I agreed, and very shortly afterwards met up with Mike Barrett, now one of our leading fight promoters but then a well-known figure in the docks as managing director of Aberdeen Wharf. Mike was sent down to a training night at the Stock Exchange to have a look at me, and he must have liked what he saw because

I became his wharf superintendent for some years, running the wharf for him until the firm moved out to Chatham. They asked me to move with them but it seemed a long way from home, so I was left to look around for another job. The Aberdeen Wharf people told me: 'Mr Gibbs, we're giving you a month's money as a golden handshake and if you find a job inside the month you still get it.'

The very next day the phone rang and it was my old boss Fred Dearsley, another great character in the docks who was a grammar school boy but an ex-Bermondsey boy as well. Fred and I had always got on and he asked me to go back to him as a ship's foreman. Naturally I grabbed at the chance and the next day told my people 'Right, I'm off.' They protested that I could not up and leave on the spot but I reminded them of our bargain, and back I went south of the river for another ten years, in fact until the wharf closed down.

Fred Dearsley would be worth a book all on his own, I reckon; he was well loved by the dockers for many years. A small man who always wore a bowler hat, he was an old type guv'nor and a very fair man. The reason he had a vacancy just at that opportune moment was that the ship worker who had the job was done for dealing in contraband stuff off the ships. So I was lucky to be available at the right time.

When New Fresh Wharf shut down I found I qualified for a pension of £3.80 a week, even though I had not paid a penny in. (Not a lot perhaps but it starts when I am 65 — which is not for a few years yet.) Short of a job yet again I pushed off to Control planning to revert back and get my book out again, only the Control manager told me I was wanted over at Tilbury by a Mr Barrett. Now this was not the boxing Barrett but another man who had been at Aberdeen Wharf, my first manager there in fact, and the dock grapevine, as efficient as jungle drums I can assure you, had told him that H. Gibbs Esq was on the hunt for work.

It felt strange moving out to the sticks. There has always been rivalry between the lads in the London Docks and those out at Tilbury. We called them carrot crunchers, swedes and other rural epithets, while the mildest thing they called us was Cockneys. But I am not the sort to worry about local rivalries, and in any case they were a hard-working crowd out at Tilbury as I discovered very rapidly. I was given no time to settle in gently. Mr Barrett called together his ship workers — and a lot of blokes were on parade because this was a big firm, Metropolitan Terminals — and told them: 'This is Harry Gibbs, he's going to be a ship worker here and I'm throwing him in the deep end. I know what he can do because he's worked with me before.' After that build-up I had to measure up, and I must have made it because I was on top wages down there right from the start. I lived in Ilford, travelling down each day and that continued until they opened up a container base in Barking and I went round to see a man called Charles St John.

He offered me a job as a supervisor but when he told me the wages I simply showed him my last wage slip and assured him he had got things round the wrong way. The problem was that they did not know enough about the docks and the clerks were getting more than the supervisors. Two weeks later he rang me back and we struck a deal. There was a few pounds difference in the wages but I was saved the trip out to Tilbury. I started as a supervisor, was soon promoted to superintendent — and I've been there ever since.

I shall always remember the first day I moved over to London Docks and joined Mike Barrett at Aberdeen Wharf. We were calling on in a street close to Rotherhithe Tunnel and calling off outside a pub round the corner. I turned up made up like Jack the Lad in a big Crombie overcoat, and everyone ignored me except one big old docker called Sid Charles. He ambled over and told me: 'I admire your pluck, son.' What he meant was that I was out of my own sector, and there was a fair bit of jealousy if you were handed a better job outside your own manor. Naturally the lads in the sector you were moving to regarded the good jobs as their own preserve.

I was there as labour master. I called off for a ship and from that day my stand used to be mobbed. They were a good bunch, there were a load of characters and quite a bit of trouble too at times. On one occasion there had been a family feud and when the labour master, not me by the way, called one bloke's name he did not step forward but pitched down at his feet. He had been done in the back with a docker's hook, something to do with wife trouble.

In the docks you rub shoulders with all sorts but do not get the idea that there are, or were, loads of villains on the wharfs. If they are there I do not know them. Particularly in the East End you hear all kinds of tales about the gangsters and bad men. Well, I never met the Kray Twins or the Richardsons, I only heard about them like everyone else. I did work for a while alongside a fellow called George Cornell who was a quiet sort of bloke, and when I heard he was shot down and killed in a pub called The Blind Beggar in Whitechapel Road I was shocked. I didn't know what George was involved in away from the docks, but I never saw any harm in him. The docks are the place for hard work, and that means there are plenty of tough men around. Thieving is inevitable, and I will talk about that in a bit, there are fights all the time, but I cannot remember any cases where a gang set on anyone.

Down on Aberdeen Wharf I was given the nickname 'Toffee', and I must admit I earned it too because I had to keep kidding the lads along to get the work done properly. I could get three ships on the berth, two on the front and one down the side of the dock. It was very hard, all piecework and I used to have to kid to them. I would put them on a promise for the next day just in order to get each day's work done. 'Are you going to put us on a split bill, Harry?' they would ask. This would mean a few extra quid for them, and I'd say 'Yes, and on top of that I'll give you a dog at New Cross tonight that's sure to win.'

I don't think it ever did win, of course, but they swallowed it, and they also believed me when I told them I definitely had another ship coming in the next morning. Very often I had no idea about the ship and when the berth was empty I would say 'Terrible thing, lads, it's got stuck in the fog out by The Needles.' After a while you could hear them say: 'Don't take a lotta notice of him, that's a load of old toffee.' It was, of course, but those lads kept coming back and earning pretty well out of the ships that did come in.

There were two paid union officials at Aberdeen Wharf and many a skirmish I had with them. One was Tom Cronin — he was awarded the OBE and you read about him quite a bit — and his pal was Freddie Bryden. I cannot remember ever winning a battle with them — they always seemed to have me over a barrel. But I do remember an occasion when at least I fought a draw.

That particular day there were two ships coming in and I found myself short of gear for unloading. I used to borrow my gear from Maltby Scrutons and they had let me down: I was supposed to have twenty scaleboards, onto which the cargo is loaded to be brought off, and I had nothing like enough. Most of those I did have were broken, but I dished them all out. Naturally the lads were upset; they wanted to receive their normal wages for piecework but would be penalised by the shortage of boards. I told them some more boards were on their way, but pretty rapidly Messrs Cronin and Bryden were sent for. Round to my office they came. 'Mr. Gibbs, you haven't got enough gear' says Cronin. 'Who says so?' I reply. 'The dockers' they said.

I tried to bluff it out, buying time after an urgent call to

Maltbys. 'Are you calling me a liar?' I said. It seems they were and they quickly took up my challenge to come round for a count-up. We reached a count of ten and, like many a fighter, I knew I was beaten, until we turned a corner and there was a real live fight in full swing. This fighter who worked in the docks, Freddie Carr his name was, was having a knuckle-up with a fellow from another ship's gang over using a crane. It was a lively scrap and Cronin says to me: 'Mr Gibbs, you haven't seen that.' 'No' I replied, 'and you've just counted up to twenty bloody scaleboards.'

Over the years I have had my fair share of punch-ups — after all you have to stand up for yourself and there are always a few occasions in the docks when respect has to be won the hard way. I remember once when promoter Barrett came perilously near to learning about throwing a punch at very close quarters. This time the 'toffee' did not work and the pair of us were left with our backs to the dock quite literally. We were surrounded by a crowd of angry dockers in no mood to listen to soft words and I wondered for a moment if we were going to wind up in the water. But we must have won the day to some extent because in the end they did not push us over.

In all the fights I have had on the stones, or the cobbles as some say, there has never been an occasion when I was two'd. By that I mean it was always man to man and never two coming at you at once. Of course there have been times when I have finished one bloke and found the next ready and waiting to step forward.

One time at Aberdeen Wharf I had a fight with a young docker after an early-morning exchange of words. As the lads turned up for work this bloke said 'Good morning Mr Sharps.' I asked the ganger 'Is he talking to you?' He assured me that the words were intended only for me. So when the gang went off to the café for a break I met them on the way back, just outside Dundee Wharf. I told this lad: 'The place to insult people is outside on the cobbles, not inside the firm where we can get the sack.' He said: 'Go away you silly old so-and-so, I'll kill you.' 'Well,' I said 'you can have the first swing. Otherwise they'll say I chinned you first.' He made his move, I chinned him and down he went under a horse and cart that was picking up stuff by the wharf. I turned my back and suddenly heard Lennie Thomas, whose brother was a Boxing Board inspector, shout 'Watch out, Harry.'

The fellow had climbed to his feet, picked up a brick and was all set to charge. I swung round as he came at me, found the target with a few more shots and down he went again. This time I left him, put on my coat and went back to work, thinking I might well be getting my cards. Later one of the main blokes from that particular gang came to see me. 'Will you give him another job tomorrow, Harry?' he asked. 'Certainly' I told him. They put the lad in an old air-raid shelter and patched him up before sending him home. After that he worked for me for a long time. He was only a youngster and far from being a bad lad.

My greatest mate in the docks was Patsy Oliffe, brother of the boxer Joe Rolfe. (Joe's real name, the family name, was Oliffe.) In the dock you always picked a buddy and got to know each other's way of working so you made a good pair on a gang. This was in the early days, of course, when I was working as a docker.

One day Patsy was handed a job while I did not get one and as I set off for Control to see if there was other work about, there was a fellow who used to be an Oxford and Bermondsey Club boy. That day he had got in first for a job. 'I done you that time,' he said. 'You shouldn't get work just because you've done a bit of boxing.' As we squared up Patsy was right there. He warned the bloke's mates to stand back and threatened to sort them out if they had a go at me. Joe Rolfe, who worked in the docks and was very well respected, was upset when he heard about the punch-up because it turned out the fellow was a cousin of his.

Nicknames abound in the docks. Apart from Toffee, I have been known as Gibbo and Gussy. Gussy seems to go with Gibbs — my father was called it and so was I when I was away in the prisoner-of-war camps. Clarkes were all called Nobby, of course, and anyone named Arthur was dubbed Teacake. I reckon that one at least was peculiar to the docks. When a docker goes up to the coffee stall and says 'cuppa coffee and halfa' he means half a toasted teacake — so all Arthurs became Teacakes.

A lot of boxers and ex-boxers work in dockland and when things were tight in the old days I must admit there were guv'nors who liked to have a ship's foreman who could fight a bit. Happily, New Fresh Wharf was not like that. We had a lot of Oxford and Bermondsey Club boys there working with us and the spirit was usually good.

Practical jokes were common, and I played a few myself. I remember the time when Lonnie Donnegan was all the rage with his skiffle and the lads felt they had to have a go themselves. When we were rained off they would slip away into this old air-raid shelter to put on a show. One had a washboard, another a tea chest with a bit of twine and another the drums. The old boy on the drums was called Monty and he must have been sixty-five if he was a day. This particular day Monty was banging away when I slipped in, whipped off the light and chucked some nails on top of his drum. I shot out and the concert broke up in uproar. Later Monty came up to me: 'Mr Gibbs,' he said, 'after what they've just done to me that group has got to find a new drummer, my music career is over.' I never let on it was me, as you can imagine.

In the old days no self-respecting docker could afford to ignore the chance to pick up something in the food line because their families had to eat, many of them were large and times were hard. But no one should get the idea that dockers are a thieving lot — how could they be in a big way when so much stuff has to be shifted through the docks?

Thieving on a small scale may be part and parcel of life to a certain extent, but there is, in fact, a high degree of honesty among dockers. I have never known anyone touch what might be called personal effects. You could leave clothing or a bag lying around and it would always be safe. And although there can always be the rascal who proves the exception to the rule, I have never known a docker deal in drugs. In fact the dockers have a rapport with the Customs' Officers and police when it comes to drugs. I am sure a great many of the tip-offs that lead to a drugs haul come from dockers because the lads feel strongly about this. A Customs' bloke will pinch a docker for buying a cheap bottle of whisky and the docker will take it in good heart because they do not have to go to court over it — they are fined on the spot down in the docks.

Dockers come in many instances from stock who had to thieve to eat, but in my experience things are not nearly so bad now as they were when I was first in the docks just after the war. Once at Aberdeen Wharf I caught a bloke stealing and I asked him if he was married. He was, with two kids. For stealing he faced instant dismissal and that would have meant him losing his book. So all I did was give him a shaking and tell him I did not want him to work for me any more and to keep off my callstand. That was to be his punishment but, lo and behold, after only a couple of weeks there he was waiting on the callstand. I gave him a job and had no more trouble with him. You really could not victimise — once you were given a name for victimising anyone you lost all your goodwill.

I am sure working in the docks has helped my refereeing. It is very much like the services: a way of life among men. Referees are there to adjudicate, and that is exactly what I have had to do so often in the docks. I am still doing it all the time. You have to control men without bullying them; no one could bully a docker, he has to be led. And there are times when they have been the most misled army of workers in the world. When I was a docker I once went on strike and found out afterwards that we had been led right up the garden path. We went out to support Canadian seamen in some inter-union row. We were out for weeks without any wages and in the end the Canadian unions simply bought each other out.

The docker is a great-hearted bloke at any time. Not so long back a man was killed at my firm. He had his leg crushed and then died in hospital. He was an old docker and well liked and when the hat went round they collected £1,000 in next to no time. What they do is give a day's wages, and then go off home as a mark of respect and lose another day's wages. When the nurses were in dispute the dockers were among the first to dip into their pockets.

Naturally they give me plenty of stick about my refereeing, and there have been lots of times when they disagree with me because many of them go boxing at the London halls. But I find them pretty fair, like with the Joe Bugner-Henry Cooper fight when I gave it to Bugner. After they had watched it on television most of them agreed — not necessarily that I was right but that the fight was close.

7

Time to Make Decisions

Did you hear about the referee who came close to recording a decision as KO'd by the ref? I doubt it, but it very nearly happened to me on one of the many occasions when I became involved in controversial, exciting or just downright funny incidents in the ring.

When people see me padding around two boxers, impassive and watchful, they may not know it but they are watching a man who is enjoying himself. I revelled in both boxing and coaching but from the start I knew I had made the right decision when I became a referee. It is for other people to evaluate how well I do the job, but over the years I can have no complaints about the invitations I have received to travel the world and gain experience. So far I have officiated in twenty-two countries, not including the British Isles, and at the last count I had refereed or judged in forty world title contests.

Lucky? Of course I am. Few referees have been more fortunate in meeting, and officiating for, men like Muhammad Ali, Joe Frazier, Sonny Liston, Sugar Ray Robinson, Emile Griffith, Carlos Monzon, Roberto Duran, Sugar Ray Leonard and a host more great champions, to say nothing of our own array of British champions.

I will not attempt to present a chronicle of my refereeing career. What I am going to do is describe some of the incidents that have happened along the way since Charlie Darby first put the germ of an idea in my mind about switching back from amateur training to becoming a professional again, this time as a referee. If I miss anyone out I apologise in advance and I may well jumble the years around a little. First of all I will stick to the British scene, but I will not keep you in suspense about that near knock-out by one burly referee.

It happened in Paris, as so much has done, but this time in a boxing ring with two of the best middleweights in the business — Carlos Monzon from the Argentine facing the hero of France Jean-Claude Bouttier. It was one hell of a world title fight.

In the eleventh round Monzon whipped over a great punch and then tried to land another as Bouttier was going down. I moved smartly enough to be right in there. I stopped his arm with one hand and with the other whipped Bouttier up from the canvas just as he started to claim a foul. I had him almost under one arm, supporting him, and as I turned round to read the riot act to Monzon, wagging my finger at him reprovingly the tip of my finger touched his cheek. Ever the actor, he reeled back as if he had been struck and I am sure that is what the crowd thought had occurred. They seemed to love it anyway.

I thought desperately, what decision do I give if he goes down and I have to count him out? Knocked out by the referee? Then the bell came to my rescue because the clock had not been stopped. A tricky situation and I was lucky it worked out OK and not KO.

Now back to the beginning, and I applied to the British Boxing Board of Control for a place on the refereeing course they advertised in Boxing News. I cannot remember anything similar in recent years, and it was a good idea. The course had a distinguished company of instructors led by the Board's then general secretary, Teddy Waltham who was at the time one of the world's leading referees, Board Steward W. Barrington Dalby and Ray Clarke, then Waltham's No. 2 and now the general secretary. 'Barry' Dalby was for many years a prominent referee but earned his real fame as a broadcaster. When title fight commentaries were on and you heard 'Now come in Barry' you knew you would receive an expert view in those very distinctive tones.

Towards the end of the course I went out to officiate for the first time in a trial bout at Wembley Town Hall, then a regular venue where promoter Eddie Durfield presented shows for years. In a trial the referee trying to earn his licence goes into the ring and handles the contest but the actual decision is given by a senior referee operating from outside the ring.

The first fight I controlled ended in a quick stoppage so I handled another later in the evening. After so many years of involvement with boxing I felt at ease when I climbed into the ring and found myself moving well, able to keep close concentration on the boxers. The referee working with me was Bill Williams, my old training colleague from Belsize days and a 'Star' official for some years. He offered advice, the best of which was to have confidence in my timekeeper. The truth of this has been brought home to me on many occasions over the years. Afterwards Eddie Durfield was kind. He told everyone he thought I would make the grade and he did a great deal for my confidence.

When my licence came through I stepped onto the bottom rung of a busy boxing scene. The three top referees in my area, the Southern Area, were Jack Hart, Tommy Little and Bill Williams and they were always at work as well as we fellows of the lower orders. Far more small halls were open then with many more tournaments in our area, outside London as well. As a 'B' referee (the lowest grading) you could reckon on working at least once a week at the height of the winter season. Not that the wages were anything exceptional. Anyone who thinks you can earn a fortune fight refereeing in this country must think again, and I am here to tell him. Still, more of money later. Suffice it to say that when I began four guineas a night was the usual fee, and I would handle two or three contests each time.

The red-letter day came on 15 April 1957 when I donned my dinner suit for the first time as a fully-fledged referee and set off for the Café Royal in London's Regent Street where, under glittering chandeliers, the National Sporting Club now present their tournaments.

After my first contest the man in charge of the Club, Mr Harding, came across for a quiet word. 'Mr Gibbs' he said, 'when you call "break" would you please remember not to shout too loud.' This was in keeping with the dignity of the NSC where the members and their guests have to observe strict silence during the rounds. Even so much as a ripple of approval or encouragement during a round brings an immediate reproof over the microphone of 'Silence please, gentlemen'.

This silence and the general atmosphere were strange at first, but now I think I prefer refereeing at the Café Royal to anywhere else — and I think they like me too because they always seem to want me there. There is a sense of tradition about the place, and no financial involvement from the audience of the kind you find in most other places, although I am sure a few side bets are struck. At the NSC the sportsmen who watch do not have a vested interest in boxing and their manners are impeccable — which is not always true of some of the other dinner-boxing clubs. They can sit back and enjoy the good things from both boxers in the ring. Impartiality is the word, and that is something every referee appreciates.

In my first year as a referee I earned £71 8s, each item faithfully recorded for me by Phyllis in a small ledger bought for the purpose. The second year brought in £62 4s 6d, including £9 14s 6d for a tournament at Folkestone where I handled every contest. During my third season I was upgraded to the 'A' category and collected a total of £168 11s. I travelled all over the area, and that is something I still do. Being a 'Star' grade referee definitely does not mean that I brandish my scorecard only at the major tournaments or plush occasions. Not only do I have to operate at every type of show, but I enjoy every time I go out.

One of my early trips out of town was to the Corn Exchange in Cambridge to referee a bloke from Bethnal Green who was fighting a black kid. The Cockney boy was definitely not in the pink of condition and after five or six rounds he began to run out of gas. Finally he went down claiming a low blow and as I was counting I whispered to him 'You're in front son, get up.' Up he climbed and when I gave the verdict to the other fellow at the end he called me a choice name.

Just like in the docks, you have to kid fighters and you have to know them, to realise when they are conning you and, most importantly, when they are really hurt or have taken sufficient punishment. Boxing hurts you know, and there is no way that can be avoided. One night at the Royal Albert Hall a young lad was having a rough time but was far from beaten when he decided to go down for a rest. I am told I was heard three rows back when I told him 'Get up son, you're not hurt.' He was so surprised he obeyed me instantly.

In London many of the small halls have closed now and their passing is a sad thing. Boxing still flourishes but the pattern has changed a great deal. No longer do the locals turn up at Shoreditch Town Hall, Manor Place Baths or even Bermondsey Baths to watch pro boxing. The trend today is more towards the dinner clubs. But those public halls were the breeding ground for London's fighters, the places where they learned their trade and were backed by their own families and supporters. Of all the halls I think Shoreditch Town Hall was my favourite, an old-fashioned hall of fading grandeur where everyone had a good view. The atmosphere there was incredible: it made fighters fight, boxers box and kept referees on their toes.

The spectators were a wonderful crowd who could read

a fight and appreciate the best in the sport. I remember One-Arm Lou, who was once one of the best known of the betting boys, cheering on a fellow he had backed at 6-4. Then the other bloke has started to do a bit and Lou had a bet on him as well. Suddenly he was asking the seconds what the fighter's Christian name was and was calling him on instead. For all the rules against betting, the chaps still call the odds around the ringside, of course, but not once in all my time as a referee have they ever approached me about a fight. A few words of self-interested advice perhaps, but no approaches.

I shall never forget the night they presented this lad from Crewe at Shoreditch. Roger Stratford was his name and the way he was milling about made me wonder if he had ever had a fight in his life. He was in with this well-taught boy from West Ham with the typical sharp style. The London lad was boxing his ears off when, suddenly, wallop and down went the home boy for the full count. You would have thought this kid had won the world championship from the roar that went up and, of course, there had to be a return because a lot of people still did not believe it. The second fight packed the place and went exactly the same way. Off went the West Hammer doing all the business and showing all the class when smash came the big punch and out he went. Young Roger was only a third-rater with nowhere to go in the game, but my word he had his two moments of glory!

The sort of contest that went down really well at Shoreditch was the Southern Area welterweight title match I refereed there between Chris Jobson from East Ham and Ivan Whiter, an Anglo-Indian boy from Tooting. They fought their hearts out and half the crowd were for one boy, half for the other. It was a great battle and no place for neutrals. I gave it to Whiter by a quarter of a point but both lads did the customers proud.

Crowd trouble at boxing is rare, I am delighted to say,

and I avoided incurring real wrath from aggrieved supporters until I handled a local derby at Wembley. Terry Spinks from West Ham, at the time a former British feather-weight champion, met Billy 'The Kid' Davis from Bow. Spinks paced his fight perfectly and won on points, on my card anyway — and that was the scoring that counted. I was a spectator when they fought a return. Tommy Little was in charge, Spinks ran out of gas and was well beaten. But the first clash brought me an enthusiastic booing and caused a rift, temporary thank goodness, between me and one of my oldest mates.

Danny Holland, the man who trained me during my brief pro career, was in Davis's corner and later in the evening we had a minor skirmish. Happily it was soon forgotten and we have remained very good friends. Danny helped Henry Cooper as trainer and cuts-man for many years until they parted late in Henry's career. In fact the night Henry lost his titles to Joe Bugner, Danny was at work in the opposite corner as his skill with injuries is always in demand.

Do not get the idea that everyone always agreed with my verdicts, or kept quiet when they did not. I had been handed a boo or two at places like Shoreditch, and one reason for this was that I did not, and still do not, give many draws. I have always felt that I am there to do a job and find a winner. Even the betting boys accept this and do not look for many drawn contests when I am in action.

I try to find a winner for every round, let alone every fight. To me it seems cowardly to give a draw, as if you lack the courage of your convictions. The only time I might begin to look for a draw is where I have two young six-rounders battling away with everything they've got. Then it seems a shame sometimes to find a winner, and you know it will make a good return anyway. Just occasionally the scoring works out unavoidably as a draw. When Bugner met the Canadian Bill Drover at the York Hall in

Bethnal Green — one of the local halls which is still flourishing — a lot of people thought Bugner won it. My score card did not agree and I surprised them by awarding a draw.

Only once in the whole of my refereeing career — at the time of writing anyway — have I been called before the Board of Control, or to be precise in this case the Southern Area Council. But it turned out to be a day with a happy ending when I presented myself at the Board's offices just off Oxford Circus.

It followed a tournament at Leyton Baths during my time as a 'B' referee and I was ordered to attend for interview. That meant I was not up on a charge but called to explain my actions, hopefully to the satisfaction of the Council. What had happened was that a boxer had been knocked down during one of the fights I had handled. He got up after a count, I ordered 'Box on' but took a second rapid glance into his eyes and before another blow could be struck I called 'Stop boxing' and ended the contest.

The Board general secretary, Teddy Waltham, was at the fight and queried me on the technical point that I should not have given the order to box on. But when we went before the Council and they heard Mr Waltham, they simply asked him why he had bothered to bring me there. All they said to me was 'Good night Mr Gibbs, your explanation has been accepted.' I was pleased enough about that, and even more delighted when I was told before I left the Board offices that I had been upgraded to the 'A' class. Another rung on the ladder and two years later, four years after first being granted my licence, I made the final step to the 'Star' grade. I believe it remains a record elevation from 'B' class to 'Star' and it opened a new world for me — quite literally because now, gradually, the invitations to officiate abroad began to come in.

Denmark will always hold a particular place in my memory. I was invited there on one of my first trips abroad to handle a show in which a team of Italian boxers took on a team of Danes — a rare type of event for professional boxing. On another occasion the Leicester manager George Biddles, who died only recently, was there to look after his boxer Wally Swift from Nottingham, a British and European champion in his day and a very cagey customer. Old George was in his corner as his boxer faced Tom Bogs, who was later to become one of the best men Denmark has produced, a European champion and world title contender. After two rounds George beckoned me over to the corner and ordered: 'Have a look at that eye.' I looked at it, amazed, and told him there was nothing there. George insisted that under Danish rules he could call the doctor, when the doctor arrived, he did his voluble best to explain the situation and it was ruled that Swift could not continue.

At the airport the next morning I bumped into George and Wally. 'You know Harry,' said George, 'we were getting £1,000 for that fight.' I told him I felt he had taken a liberty. 'Well,' replied Biddles, 'he is only a middleweight fighting a light-heavy.' George, who took Hogan 'Kid' Bassey to the world featherweight title and Jack Bodell and Richard Dunn to the British and European heavyweight titles, knew every trick in the book and was clever with it. He knew the game backwards and I cannot remember him ever allowing one of his fighters to take a good hiding.

Over the years I found myself involved in a clash or two with Teddy Waltham. One incident followed a featherweight match at the Royal Albert Hall involving Frankie Taylor, one of our best young fighters never to win a pro title, and a South American named Harold Gomes. For nine rounds Gomes was licking the pants off Frankie but then Taylor, who was aptly nicknamed 'Tiger', caught him with a succession of good punches and down he went.

As Gomes regained his feet I heard the bell, and there is no doubt in my mind that if I did not actually hear *the* bell I did hear *a* bell. I sent them to their corners and as I walked across the ring ready to mark my scorecard I heard the timekeeper, the late Stan Courtney, say 'Harry, there are still thirteen seconds of the round remaining.' I told him to treat it as a completed round, and was highly relieved when Frankie kept up the assault in the next round and stopped Gomes. If Gomes had lasted out there is no way Taylor could have been given the verdict because he was so far behind on points. Funnily enough I believe Frank, now boxing writer for *The People* admits he was concussed from early in the fight and remembers nothing about the incident. In fact he did not know the result until he was told later in the dressing room.

As I climbed out of the ring Waltham claimed me: he appeared to think it was my fault and I assured him that I had heard a bell. I suppose one of the betting boys could have reached over and touched the bell while everyone's attention was on the action, but Stan — the best time-keeper I have worked with by the way — assured me his bell did not sound. Next morning the newspapers all wrote about the phantom bell. They even suggested there was a fire engine roaring past the Albert Hall, but it was never solved neither did I find a satisfactory explanation. Luckily, Teddy Waltham did not pursue the matter further either.

Taylor was eventually forced to retire early because of eye trouble but not without sharing in one of the best contests I have ever handled. On an April night in 1963 he came face to face at the Royal Albert Hall with Lennie 'The Lion' Williams — The Lion v the Tiger, both unbeaten and sensational performers.

Williams, the nineteen-year-old from South Wales, damaged the twenty-year-old Taylor (who won a European amateur title boxing for his hometown club in Lancaster) around the eyes but I defy anyone to tell me who was in front after five rounds. It was action from both boys right from the start. There was no official title at stake — only pride and those unbeaten records. The tension built up to a tremendous level, and then Taylor, magnificently fit, took over in the sixth. He began to find his way through Williams's guard with ferocious punches and finally unleashed a left hook and right cross that sent The Lion to the floor for me to count him out. A great fight, and a return was inevitable. I was not the man in charge but I saw Taylor win more easily with Williams not showing quite the same edge as he had on the first occasion.

The first time I stepped into a ring to control a British title fight was when I travelled to Cardiff for the featherweight match between Howard Winstone and Harry Carroll in May 1962. Winstone won in six rounds and I have always admired him as one of the best British fighters of my time so far as pure boxing goes. He had a beautiful left hand and all the moves, real class. I always thought Terry Spinks was a talented performer, but I saw Winstone beat him. Howard was a perfect gentleman in the ring and full of courage too, as I discovered when I refereed him against Jimmy Anderson. Jimmy carried a proper whack on him and put Winstone on the deck inside the first round. It was quite a shock but Howard climbed up and boxed his ears off.

My first world title contest, a nerve-testing occasion, brought me into contact with a man who was a complete master of his art — Emil Griffith, one of the finest boxers the world has seen, champion in his day at both welter and middleweight and a worthy candidate for the Hall of Fame. In September 1964 Griffith came to the Empire Pool — as the Wembley Arena was known then — to defend the welter crown against Brian Curvis, a dapper stylist from Wales. I was nervous to say the least, but lucky to start with such a clear-cut fight. That night I felt just as much on edge as I did before a fight when I was boxing myself. If I went for a pee once I went ten times, and when I stood in the corner I felt I wanted to go again!

Early on, around the second I think, I stood in a neutral corner marking my card when I felt a tug at my trouser leg. It was a TV technician who ordered: 'Move into the other corner between rounds.' I informed him, forcibly, that it was my job to adjudicate a world title fight not to produce Sportsview.

Certainly I had no problem picking out the winner. Griffith was the guv'nor and finished comfortably ahead over the fifteen rounds, although it was always a fine fight. Curvis did his utmost, but the other fellow was just that bit too good all along the line. It was a clean scrap and if my memory is right I issued only one real warning, and that was to Curvis for misuse of the head which might well have been accidental. I only remember that incident so well because I still have a picture of me warning Brian.

I have handled contests involving Griffith on a number of occasions over the years and, amazingly, he has not been retired all that long. On one occasion he met Tom Bogs in Copenhagen and Griffith, who liked to inject some humour into a contest, was playing around more than usual. Finally, I moved over to his corner where Gil Clancy, the famous American manager and cornerman, was looking after him. 'Now look, son' I warned him, 'if you don't buck your ideas up I'll throw you out for not trying.' I did Bogs no favour at all: in the next round Griffith went to work and the Dane had to be rescued before it ended.

I met Emil again when I went to Monte Carlo for the world middleweight title fight between Rodrigo Valdes and Benny Briscoe, which was one of the best I have handled because the action was simply superb. In 1979 we met again in Puerto Rico when he was in the corner with Wilfredo Benitez in a world welter fight against Carlos Palomino, the boy who took the world title from John H. Stracey. That time Emil had wanted to give me the gloves as a memento of the fight, only someone stole them and ruined his plan.

A Cold Stare for Ali

At a time when we are producing so many fine fighters at other weights, the decline of heavyweight boxing in recent years is both sad and surprising. I know we have heard so often about Britain's 'horizontal heavyweights' but that is in many ways a load of old bull. We may not have set the world alight but until the last few years there have always been heavyweight matches to sell out the halls and catch the public's imagination.

For many people there is nothing like a heavyweight match to stir them up, even though the connoisseurs might plump for smaller men. I can look back to a whole series of stirring contests involving men like Henry Cooper, Brian London, Joe Bygraves, Joe Bugner, Billy Walker, Jack Bodell and Johnny Prescott. Sadly it is some time since I handled a real cracker between British heavies and I look forward eagerly to the day when the big men come back. When I see those hefty rugby players thumping each other around I am amazed that more of them do not try their luck in the boxing ring, particularly when everyone knows it is the heavies who attract some of the biggest purses.

What I would like to do here is jump back over the years and recall just a few of the heavyweight clashes in this country that stick in my mind — and later, undoubtedly, I shall think of many more that should have been listed. But this lot will do for starters I can tell you, particularly when Billy Walker was involved.

Billy was one of the gamest boys I have ever seen: he took one punch, or sometimes two or three, to get in with one of his own and I am delighted to see him looking so well today. Excitement, or the anticipation of it, is what brings in the crowds, and Billy certainly generated plenty of that; win or lose he always delivered the goods. He never won a title, but he put up a brave battle the night he challenged Cooper at Wembley in 1967. Henry won in six rounds and earned his third Lonsdale Belt outright at the same time.

The night I refereed Walker's fight with the old warrior Joe Bygraves, at Olympia I believe, I should not in fact have been doing the job because Tommy Little had been appointed. But he had pulled out as part of a protest against the low fees being paid to referees and the Boxing Board ordered me to take over, which at the time meant a fee of eighteen guineas. When I realised what the situation was I wanted to pull out and not be involved in the dispute one way or the other, but Ray Clarke, then the Board's assistant secretary, warned me that it was a Board instruction that I take the job. I did not want to fall out with them so I went ahead, although I do have some strong views about referees' fees for major contests.

The fight itself was a titanic struggle and I was forced to give Joe several warnings for punching low. Finally he chucked one in that seemed a blatant foul to me and I had to throw him out, regretfully I must add because he was a fine fighter and there was very little in the contest at the time.

The second time Walker met the Birmingham boy Johnny Prescott, I was in charge at Wembley. In their first scrap Tommy Little had stopped it in Walker's favour and the conflict ebbed and flowed furiously in the return. These two magnificently fit young prospects fought their hearts out and at the end I awarded it to Prescott by a whisker, lifting his arm as he swayed wearily in the centre of the ring. Prescott had been felled for eight in the third but fought his way back in the later rounds to snatch the decision in a fight that was rich in sportsmanship as well as in thrills.

When it was announced some time afterwards that I had been nominated to handle Billy's fight with the former British champion Brian London — with whom I had a few amateur adventures in Italy you may remember — there was an immediate protest, but it did not come from the Walker camp. It was Al Phillips, London's manager, who sounded off. One reporter recorded that Al made the telephone unnecessary as he roared his protest from Blackpool, Brian's hometown where he was training. Al stressed that he had nothing against me personally but he was incensed that the Board's Southern Area Council had appointed a Londoner to handle the fight: it was North v South battle and the referee should come from outside those areas. I said nothing at all, and Ray Clarke merely stated that my appointment had been the 'unanimous' decision of the Board and would not be changed.

Billy Walker, training at Pitsea in Essex, made no complaints. 'Gibbs will do me fine — even if he did give Johnny Prescott the verdict in our second fight' was his comment. His brother George, who was also his manager, scorned any idea of a protest: 'That referee will suit me because he has the courage of his convictions,' he said.

The Walkers did not moan about the Prescott decision, but then they were never cry-babies whichever way the decision went. And I can never remember them criticising a referee. For the record I gave this verdict to London on points after he had used his vast experience to outsmart Billy, for all his enthusiasm and courage. All round, Billy did not have much luck when I refereed him and he was a loser once again when he met Jack Bodell at Wembley. That turned out to be a sensational battle with both men on the brink of defeat several times before I finally felt obliged to rescue Billy in the eighth round.

The Press were never very kind to Jack Bodell, the 'swineherd from Swadlincote' as they called him. He was a southpaw and looked clumsy, but he had a number of things going for him. Firstly he was a lot better than people imagined, secondly he could punch harder than most and thirdly his career was being guided by that wily old customer George Biddles, of whom I have spoken before.

From the start Jack stuck his southpaw right jab in Billy's face and after jabbing him dizzy knocked him down for eight. The second round was even worse for Walker and when a left felled him again he cracked his head on the canvas. I watched him carefully, but Billy was always remarkably strong and climbed up to weather the storm. Even so I was amazed when he came out like a whirlwind in the third, and I reckon Jack was just as surprised. Now it was his turn to take a battering and finally Walker chinned him. Down went Bodell and as he fell his head became cushioned on the bottom rope. This seemed to shake him round: he was up at nine and in a position to defend himself as Billy got stuck in. You know, I reckon he missed Jack with just about every punch from then on in that round and simply could not press home his advantage. Billy had run out of steam as he made his bid. In the next he was in terrible trouble. Down he went once more and although this remarkably brave man levered himself up again I had to step in within seconds.

One of the toughest heavyweight fights I have handled — at least according to the build-up propaganda — involved Brian London and an American named Tom McNeeley. McNeeley arrived with a rugged reputation. He was billed as a rough, tough longshoreman from Boston who threw the rule book out of the ring if he had the chance. Needless to say I did not want him to have any chance, and when he visited one of the London small halls during his training here he saw me sling a lad out, disqualify him. The Press wrote 'Harry Gibbs has next week's fight, and McNeeley has already had a taste of the way he works.'

Even so when they came out like billy goats in the first

three rounds I was loath to pull them up too sharply, and I
really was in a difficult spot. Immediately before the heavyweight match Jack Hart had given a controversial verdict
in a Howard Winstone fight against an American, Don
Johnson I think. The crowd were doing their best to
raise the roof and I could not afford to chuck anyone out
early because I am sure they would have torn the place
apart.

So for the first three rounds they transgressed the rules
with what was for me only mild reproof. At one point in
the first or second London said to me 'He's butting me,
Harry.' I told him 'Well butt him back.' Once the crowd
had quietened the time soon arrived to take a grip and I
called them together. 'That's enough, lads' I warned. 'Any
more of it and out you go, one or both of you I don't
care which.' Happily they recognised the storm signals and
obeyed, and London went on to win clearly. He was a very
good fighter on his day, particularly when he was on top.

In 1959 London fought Floyd Patterson for the world
title in Indianapolis, flying out against the wishes of the
British Board who later fined him heavily. He was knocked
out in eleven rounds, but kept his career going so success-
fully that seven years later he was given the chance to
challenge Muhammad Ali at Earls Court.

The fight took place in August 1966, only three months
after Henry Cooper had challenged Ali at Highbury and
been beaten on cuts. I was appointed to referee, under
British rules without judges to share in the decision making.
It was my second world title fight in six weeks because I
was in charge at the Royal Albert Hall when Scotland's
Walter McGowan beat Salvatore Burruni of Italy for the
World Boxing Council's flyweight title. That is another
story and for the present I am concentrating on heavyweights. Who better than the remarkable Muhammad Ali,
first seen in Britain as Cassius Clay when Henry chinned
him at Wembley Stadium but still lost on cuts?

I refereed on the bill that night, although not for very long. I handled the heavyweight match between Jimmy Ellis and the Tongan Johnny Halafihi and after Jimmy dropped him twice in the first round I soon stopped it. Ellis went on to win the world title, or a version of it at least. That night I rated him a better prospect than Clay who, as you will remember vividly I am sure, found himself in all kinds of desperate trouble when Henry's hammer cracked him on the whiskers.

The night Cooper received his second chance, this time with the world title on the line, I was once again refereeing on the programme. This gave me another chance to see Ali before I refereed him myself.

Ali and his people accepted the British rules completely, although we did have an exchange in the dressing room when I went to outline what was expected. When foreign fighters are involved referees in this country visit each fighter to make sure the rules are thoroughly understood. When I went in to see Ali with the Board's chief inspector Harry Vines, he started to turn on some of his chatter. 'Now look Mr Referee' he said, with those eyes of his rolling, 'I hear this guy hits to the kidneys and butts.' I gave Ali one of my coldest stares. 'Right, sonny' I told him, 'You do your job and I'll do mine.' If I am honest I think I put it a trifle stronger than that but I will leave that to your imagination.

Poor old Brian was not given much time to bend or twist the rules, let alone break them. The fight had been going about seven minutes before Ali threw in a flurry of punches in a corner and London sank to the canvas for me to count him out. I must say it did not look as if he had been hurt all that badly, but who are we to know how hard Ali could hit? In his time he has produced all sorts of strange punches to win fights, like when he fought Liston the second time and it looked as if Sonny simply went down as quickly as he could. Ali told the world he used a special new punch, although that night I do not think he knocked anyone out. So far as London is concerned I believe it is unfair to him to say that his heart was not in it. I feel the problem may well have been stagefright. He had been psyched by Ali — and in his time Ali has psyched a whole lot of good fighters.

Ali did so much to heighten interest in boxing that it is a tragedy he carried on far too long, in fact until he was in danger of actually damaging the sport. The lack of effective world control meant he was able to box on, and I can tell you I would now refuse to referee or judge one of his fights, were I to be invited and were the Board of Control to permit me. I have never had the chance to get to know Ali well, but I have always found him brash and he was certainly a tricky, cheeky customer. Teddy Waltham told me once of the night he refereed Ali's world defence against Karl Mildenberger in Germany. He warned Ali for hitting with the open glove and the champion asked him 'Which hand, ref?'

Now Joe Frazier is a fellow I have always preferred — not so much as a fighter but as a perfect gentleman, in fact to use an American expression a real nice guy. I refereed Joe against Joe Bugner at Earls Court and when he caught Bugner with a cracking left hook it had a slightly delayed effect. Bugner was sinking to the canvas rather than crashing when I shouted 'Step back'. Instead of taking a liberty and whipping in another punch to finish it, Frazier obeyed me instantly and stepped back. Those are the moments that a referee always remembers. Frazier was lucky in the fight: his eye was so badly closed up that if it had been over fifteen rounds instead of twelve I do not think he would have finished it.

That, for me, was the best performance of Bugner's career. He was a boy who promised a vast amount but usually delivered rather less than his potential. He shook Frazier soon after going down himself and although he was way behind on my card he came back strongly. I remember thinking I might have a problem. People watching a grandstand finish tend to forget what has happened in the early rounds, and this is duly recorded on a referee's scorecard. Once an underdog fights back he immediately captures the hearts of an English crowd.

Apart from his brave fight back against Frazier I can only remember one occasion when Bugner looked to me as if he was relishing going in for a battle. That was when he met Richard Dunn, the red headed Yorkshireman who late in his career struck a golden vein, once again thanks in con siderable part to that wily old Svengali from Leicester, George Biddles.

Richard won the British and European titles and then challenged Muhammad Ali disastrously in Munich. He was big and brave, an experienced pro, but not really able to take too much on the chin. Anyway he was matched with Bugner at Wembley and the place was packed. I had the refereeing job and I must admit I was astonished by the way Bugner went about his business. It is the only time that I can remember when he came out steaming for a fight. Richard was amazed too, I am sure, and soon collected a good one that put him on the floor clawing at Bugner's knees. The third time he went over I counted him out and as I signalled the 'out' my hand just touched side of his head as he tried to haul himself upright. In some of the pictures it looked as if I was giving him a back hander. The next week I went over to Germany to referee and some joker came leaping up with one of the pictures in a newspaper. 'Mr Gibbs,' he said, 'it seems as if you knock them out as well as count them out!'

9

Sorry Henry - But I was in Charge

The saddest decision I have ever had to make as a referee cost Henry Cooper the British, European and Commonwealth heavyweight titles, and to my sorrow seems to have started a feud that lingers on even now. Harry Gibbs v Henry Cooper is the confrontation that has built up ever since that momentous night in 1971 when I added up my scores and lifted Joe Bugner's right arm to cost 'Our 'Enry' those titles he valued so highly.

It was a sad moment for Henry, for his millions of supporters and, let me stress, for referee Gibbs. Not only had I been a Cooper admirer for years but so had my family. When I walked indoors that night Phyllis said: 'It must have been very close, the radio commentator gave it a draw.'

Naturally sentiment has no place in a referee's mind — or it certainly should not have — and all I had done was my job. A thousand times since, and probably more, I have been over that fight, which is still crystal-clear in my mind and all I can say is that I would always have given the same verdict.

I have no regrets then for the decision, only for the fact that it had to be Henry. Let me say at once that I have never regarded myself as being involved in a feud with Henry Cooper, his manager, the late Jim Wicks, or anyone to do with them. What their view is I cannot say, but I will always be sad that a decision given honestly after a desperately close fight has led to so much controversy and bitterness.

When I told my friends I was going to set down a few

reminiscences in a book, the reaction of several was immediate: 'The Cooper fight will make a good opening chapter' they said, but that is certainly not my view of it. The Bugner-Cooper episode takes its proper place in my story, although I will expand on it because it has caused such a huge amount of discussion even, I suspect, among people who didn't see the fight either at Wembley or on television.

One thing I do feel is that I would not want the refereeing career of Harry Gibbs to be remembered for just one verdict, even if it did signal the end of his career for a man who was fast becoming a folk hero in his own time.

In writing about the fight I must get one thing straight. I will tell you about it and give my views but I am not attempting to justify myself. I respect the many people who did not agree with me and on the other hand I am grateful that quite a few went my way too. For all the fuss and bother, I was never so much as questioned by the Board of Control about the decision, and it never damaged my career for a single instant. I have handled two score of world title fights since and have been in regular demand all over the world.

Nor did it damage Cooper as I see it, except that it dented his pride. He has never looked back since. He was ready to retire, in fact he would probably never have fought again, and the way the whole affair developed only increased public interest in him and sympathy for him. His present career right in the centre of public life may well have been helped, and certainly has not been hindered, by the way his fighting career ended. Only when I felt my own reputation was at stake after reading a section of Henry's book did I take legal action. I did so with great reluctance and not to win punitive damages. I won the case, received a public apology and for my part that was the end of the matter.

I have refereed thousands of contests but whether I

like it or not the title match I handled on 16 March 1971 turned out to be the most controversial of the lot. Yet when I was given the news of my appointment I was delighted: it was a landmark in my refereeing career, which at that stage was building up pretty well in any case. The fight seemed to me to have all the ingredients for a classic and I knew I would have to be right on the top line handling a match between an up-and-coming 'golden boy' and a man who was already a national figure and incredibly popular all over Britain. I had refereed both of them before, in fact on a number of occasions, and certainly had no inkling of the storm a decision one way or other would cause, although I certainly found out with a vengeance later. I suppose I had refereed Cooper five or six times previously and Bugner in quite a few of his fights on the way up. I remember handling three Cooper fights at the Royal Albert Hall where he lost the lot, although without any great controversy that I can recall.

I had no affiliation with either camp, of course, and no antagonism either. There was a spell when I was in dispute with Danny Holland, who acted as Cooper's trainer for many years, but that was soon over. Danny is a very dear friend of mine, in fact he trained me when I was fighting professional, and in any case he had left the Cooper camp before this contest. As for Jim Wicks, who was one of boxing's greatest characters and eighty-six when he died in 1980, I had few dealings with him although I was actually born in the street in Bermondsey where he used to live during his early life. His son Jackie, who works for promoter Harry Levene, was a friend of mine and when the National Sporting Club held an evening to honour Henry some time before the Bugner fight, I received an invitation. So I do not think anyone could say I had any bias against Henry.

When the Bugner fight arrived Henry was thirty-six years old, an ageing warrior perhaps but I reckon he was a far better fighter in his latter years than when he first began as a pro. I think his resurgence may have started when he was knocked down by the powerful Welsh fellow Dick Richardson, got up and did him in style with his left hook. Henry's hammer was a ferocious weapon and he did not look back after that. Still, if you take a look over his career you will see he was an in and out sort of boxer who weathered the bad patches, aided by the forceful guidance of Jim 'The Bishop' Wicks, and finally earned himself a fortune. I reckon Henry was right when he told people he was like good wine which matures the older it gets.

But whatever setbacks he may have had, Henry was the boy who chinned Cassius Clay, the Louisville Lip, at Wembley Stadium – slammed him over with that left hook and very nearly knocked him clean out. Only the bell rescued Clay, and then came one of boxing's great mysteries when the American's glove was discovered to be split and there was a long break between rounds, giving him a lot more time in which to recover. I was refereeing on the bill that night, and I can shed some light on the mystery of how the glove came to be the centre of controversy immediately after Clay's wavering progress back to his corner.

The timekeeper was Stan Courtney, a close friend of mine who later wrote to Boxing News to tell them the exact time it took before the next round started. But Stan always maintained that the glove was split the round before, attention called to it and a new glove sent for from the dressing rooms which are a long way from the middle of the stadium. While the new glove was on its way, down went Clay in one of the most dramatic rounds of all time in British boxing, leaving Henry on the brink of a sensational victory.

Now, I am well aware that Clay's trainer Angelo Dundee is reputed by some to have slit his man's glove to play for time. I think at this long range Angelo even likes to perpetuate a touch of intrigue about it, but cute as he is I do not believe he would go to such lengths. In any case he could have had no idea before that round started just what terrible trouble his brash young star would run into. So, if Stan is correct, the problem can only have been caused by a fault in the glove itself.

There is some doubt, too, over whether the glove was ever actually changed. The late Dick Reekie, who was in Clay's corner, always insisted that the referee George Smith finally ordered him to box on with the old glove. On the other hand, Harry Vines, who is now the British Board's chief inspector and was the man who fetched the fresh pair of gloves from the dressing rooms, is adamant that a changeover was made. Whatever the truth, there is no doubt that Dundee made a meal of the affair — as any good second would — while his fighter's buzzing head cleared. Then Clay went back to work and Henry's cuts finally defeated him.

Even so, Cooper's reputation was made and when Clay, now calling himself Muhammad Ali, defeated Sonny Liston to take the world title he came back to London to give Henry another go. This time the Arsenal football ground at Highbury was the venue and again I was refereeing on the bill. There was no high drama from Henry but a really good performance before those terrible cuts stopped him yet again. Ali has never forgotten the way Cooper belted him over and I have heard him say he has never been hit harder. But for the bell and then the damaged glove giving him a stay of execution, the whole pattern of heavyweight boxing might have been altered.

When Henry arrived finally at the Bugner defence it brought one of those big nights true boxing followers love. Wembley Arena was packed, the atmosphere electric, expectant. For my part I did not feel under any extra pressure, just that touch of nervousness I welcome because it keeps me on my toes.

Right: Mother and Father
Gibbs — Nellie and the
redoubtable Gus.

Below: All smiles on
repatriation day — I am
fourth from the right in
the back row. (Photo:
The Times)

Left: Culture, too, with Shakespeare at the Oxford and Bermondsey Club — and I play Mowbray.

Below: Spot the British champions in this 1953 England squad. Among them are flyweight Frankie Jones, featherweight Dave Charnley, middleweight Ron Barton, light-heavyweight Henry Cooper and heavyweight Joe Erskine.

Above: Family group — in the back garden with my wife Phyllis and daughter Sheila. (*Photo: The Sun*)

Right: Proud Grandad with Nicola and Matthew.

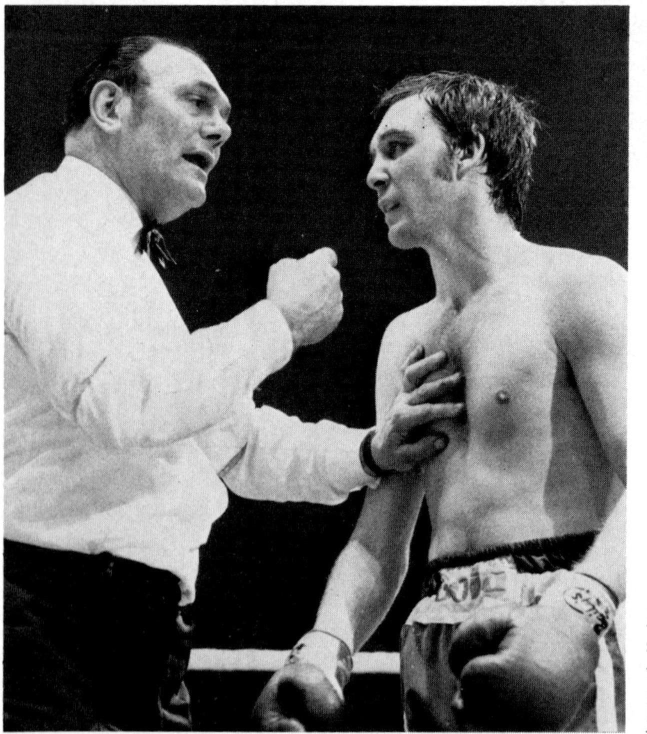

Above: 'What am I bid?' Getting to work for charity by auctioning some autographed gloves. (*Photo: RGL Photography Ltd*)

Left: 'Now watch it, son' — dishing out a warning to John H. Stracey. (*Photo: Daily Mirror*)

Gangway for a referee — moving in to part John Conteh and Jorge Ahumada during their world light-heavyweight title match at Wembley. Conteh won on **points**.
(Photo: Daily Mirror)

Left: Enough is quite enough — stepping in to the rescue and Frankie Taylor has won another fight.

Below: 'Now wait just a moment, lads' — keeping former British feather-weight champion Vernon Sollas (on the left) and his opponent apart, briefly, at the Royal Albert Hall. (*Photos: Daily Mirror*)

Above: Mark Rowe, the former British middleweight champion, gets up with an eye on his waiting opponent. I seem to be looking watchful too.

Below: A sell-out night at Wembley Arena. Dave 'Boy' Green goes in headfirst against John H. Stracey.

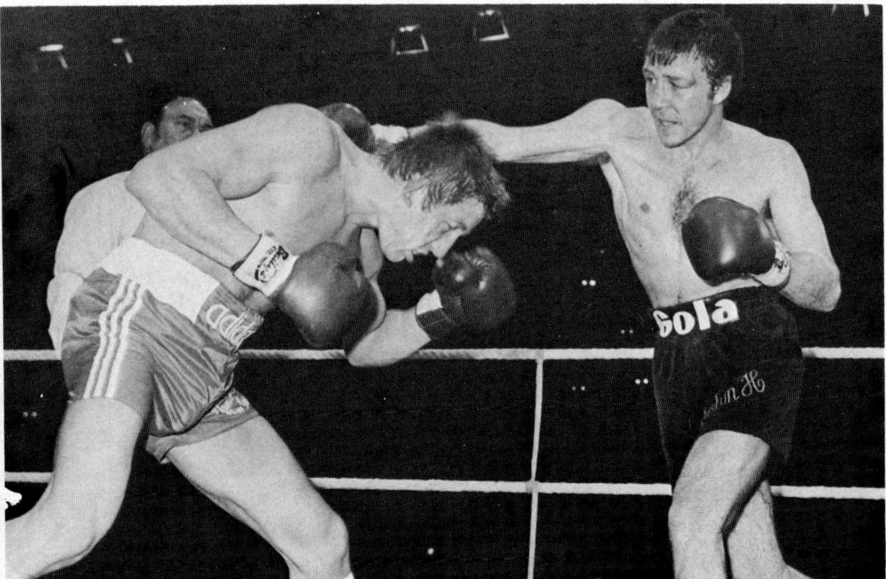

Left: Counting out Brian London while Muhammad Ali waits expectantly, if casually, in a neutral corner. (*Photo: Syndication International*)

Below: Summit meeting in Zambia — with President Kenneth Kaunda.

Joe Bugner and Joe Frazier battle it out at Earls Court, and in this picture Bugner looks confident. (*Photo: Sport and General Press Agency*)

Left: 'You must mind your head, son' — I warn Welshman Brian Curvis during his world welter challenge against the great Emile Griffith. Emile rubs his head, just to indicate exactly where he was hurt. (*Photo: Daily Mirror*)

Below: 'Whoops, ho up Hedgemon.' I he a sagging Hedgemon Lewis back to the corner after the American has been stopped by the then world welterweight champion John H. Stracey.

Billy Walker clutches his midriff as he runs into trouble against Jack Bodell. (*Photo: Daily Mirror*)

'The winner' — and up goes Alan Rudkin's arm at the Royal Albert Hall.

'Nine and out' — Lennie 'The Lion' Williams's gallant fight against Frankie Taylor in their first meeting comes to an end as I count the Welshman out. (*Photo: Daily Mirror*)

In the ring I am sure my mind was completely open — indeed I hope it always is when I am refereeing. I set out to control the contest just as I would any six-rounder. It was not Henry Cooper the champion against Joe Bugner the challenger, but two pairs of shorts. Reputations counted for nothing, and do not forget that in this country a challenger does not have to produce something out of the ordinary to wrench away a title. Whoever is in front at the end is the winner, there is no leaning towards a champion but on the other hand no leaning the other way in an attempt to be over-fair.

The pattern of the contest remains clear in my mind even now. Bugner, big, blond and powerful — although it was power he never really used to its full potential — made all the play in the early rounds. Henry seemed very lethargic and did not come into it until about the ninth round when he put in several more good rounds. As a contest it did not turn out to be a classic. In fact it was a rather scrambling affair which only came alive when Cooper found his touch. Then it livened up and the tension increased as the fight built up to its climax. I felt that Joe started to lose concentration at one point, regained his poise to keep several rounds level and then pulled out the stops in the final three minutes.

I am sure a great many of those who saw the contest felt sympathetic towards Cooper. After all he was a good champion who was deservedly popular and many of those watching may have been looking to mark rounds in his favour. On the other hand I was the professional referee whose job it was to adjudicate without regard for anything except the contest as it developed.

Round by round the scores went down on my card. I scored each round exactly as I saw it and at the end of the fourteenth I had them dead level. I totted up that card two or three times to make sure I was right. 'Whoever I give it to I'm going to get a booing,' I thought. 'But whoever wins it is going to get it.' I have always felt that at the end of fifteen rounds a referee who cannot find a winner is not worth his salt, although a draw is possible and this one could not have been closer. All of which made me very much the man in the hot seat.

Those were the days when we scored each round out of five with quarter points, and my eyes ran up and down the columns on my card to check my fractions. I must be honest, another thought flashed across my mind. I thought 'Thank God Cooper's an old pro, surely he must have saved something for the last round.' Stan Courtney rang the bell, 'Fifteenth and final round', and out they came to settle it. I am sure any unbiased observer would agree that no way did Henry win that last round. It was Bugner putting on the pressure, slamming forward with a final fling that gave me no option.

As the bell ended it, Henry turned to me and held out his hand. After all he was an old campaigner. But I had to turn away and go to Bugner to lift his arm. Anyone who saw the fight or watched it later on television must have seen, too, that Henry appeared to accept it, that is until Jim Wicks and others round him started up. Anyway that is my feeling.

The crowd reaction in protest was predictable, and as I remember it not particularly hostile despite the boos. Henry was London's idol and I suppose seventy-five per cent of those in the hall came to see him win. There was a fair amount of clapping at the ringside along with the boos, and immediately I climbed down from the ring Larry Gains, the old Commonwealth heavyweight champion, came up and said 'Mr Gibbs, that was a very fair and just decision. I admire you for it.'

Harry Carpenter, who was doing the television commentary for BBC, made Cooper a clear winner, but the millions who listened on radio were not given the idea that the champion was romping away with it. I have not only heard the commentary on tape, but have a copy of part of it. The blow-by-blow commentator was Simon Smith with Fred Verlander putting in the inter-round summaries. Verlander, scoring it round by round as it happened and keeping his live audience in touch as the fight developed, made the fight a draw.

After Smith had described the excitement of the final round Verlander summed up: 'I in fact gave the last round to Bugner' he said, 'and that made the score absolutely even, and I wouldn't like to argue in any way whatever with Harry Gibbs's scorecard. I don't know what his final result will be but I evened it up so much that I gave it 73¼ to each boxer.' In fact my scoring was 73¾ to Bugner, 73½ to Cooper — a difference of a quarter of a point. I would not argue with Verlander's estimate and from what I heard he did not argue with mine. The difference was that I was the man appointed to name the winner.

Have I ever made a mistake with a verdict? Well, I never have in my opinion but all referees are human. This fight was judged under the old system of five marks to the winner of the round, scaled down to four and threequarters and four and a half. If a round was level it was five-five, if one man took the round by a little then he received five and his opponent four and threequarters. If he won well, like having a ten yards lead after a 100 yards sprint, he took the round by half a point. In your column on the scorecard you marked down the advantage point: one for a quarter, two for a half and three for threequarters, splitting a whole one up into four. A quarter-point was the smallest margin by which a fight could be won. Today the quarters have gone and we judge in halves with ten marks to the winner, otherwise the system is the same.

There was no real trouble round the ring afterwards. I was not conscious that I needed any special police escort and later Stan Courtney and I walked out of the hall together. Certainly there were boos and one or two people abused me but you expect that when a title fight as important as this one has turned on a knife edge. A few in the crowd shouted 'fix' but I have never bent a fight in my life and have heard all that kind of thing before. I was not surprised during the fight if the crowd roared whenever Henry looked like throwing a punch, let alone landing one. I was being paid to put all that out of my mind, and in fact you do not hear a great deal of it because your attention is entirely focused on the contest.

Danny Holland came over and asked 'All on the last round, wasn't it Harry?' I told him that was exactly the way I had seen it. Then Colin Hart of *The Sun* told me he made Bugner win and would stand up and be counted. But Press opinion in the main went Cooper's way and one or two thought he won clearly. Peter Wilson of *The Mirror* certainly did, but Peter remains a good friend of mine. We do not see him at the ringside so often now that he is semi-retired but he always talks to me when we meet. In fact he invited me to his farewell party when he retired from full-time work.

Jim Wicks said nothing to me and although I have heard and read since that he had to be held back in the ring, I was not aware of it. As soon as I had held up Bugner's hand my job was to complete my card and leave the ring. Referees are not there to be noticed when they have finished their work.

As I said, I doubt if the result harmed Henry apart from his professional pride — which naturally meant a lot to him. But think of the publicity and sympathy he received from people who thought, and probably still think, he was given a raw deal. A return fight would have been a sell-out, but Cooper stuck to his decision to retire. Andy Smith, Bugner's manager, told me that Bugner had offered a return but it never took place — perhaps the terms were not right.

The bitterness that has come into the whole affair has surprised me. You never hear me running Cooper down, why ever should I? But I do wish he had been man enough to accept the decision however much he felt that he had won. Without knowing for sure of course, my feeling is that Henry himself would have accepted graciously if it had not been for others around him.

After the contest I was asked to go on television when the film was shown the next night. They rang me in the docks at Tilbury to ask me, but I refused. The Board of Control would have taken a dim view if I had gone in front of the cameras. What I did do was to demand that the fight be shown in its entirety so that people could judge for themselves — as far as you ever can from television — which they definitely could not do from highlights. Later in the day the BBC issued a statement saying the contest would be shown in full.

My brother rang when I got home from work. 'Is that you Harry?' he said. 'They've got newspaper placards out in the City saying "Referee demands trial by public" and I guessed that was you.' In the docks the feeling seemed to be that if Harry Gibbs had given it against Cooper, who after all came from just about the same manor as himself, then Cooper must have been beaten. This feeling intensified after they had seen the fight for themselves. More and more came up, not all to say I was right of course, but that at the very least it had been desperately close. What most said was that they didn't see what all the fuss was about. A lot had watched the film with the sound turned off. I've sat and watched fights and listened to the commentary and although they are great lads, sometimes I think it is best to make up your own mind.

With the Board making no move to even ask me about the decision — I would have been most upset if they had, incidentally — that was the end of it officially. But if I said it did not shake me up I would be telling a lie.

REFEREE'S SCORE SHEET

No. 3

Date 16·3·71 No. of Rounds 15

Promoter HARRY·LEVINE

Venue WEMBLEY·POOL

Referee HARRY·GIBBS

HENRY·COOPER v. JOE·BUGNER

Total Marks	Advantage	Score	Round	Score	Advantage	Total Marks	Remarks
4¾		4¾	1	5	1	5	
9½		4¾	2	5	1	10	
14½	1	5	3	4¾		14¾	
19¼		4¾	4	5	1	19¾	
24½	1	5	5	4¾		24½	
29		4¾	6	5	1	29½	
34		5	7	5		34½	
39		5	8	5		39½	
43¾		4¾	9	5	1	44½	
48¾		5	10	5		49½	
53¾		5	11	5		54½	
58¾	1	5	12	4¾		59¼	
63¾	1	5	13	4¾		64	
68¾	1	5	14	4¾		68¾	
73½		4¾	15	5	1	73¾	

Winner BUGNER

Referee's Sig. H. W. Gibbs

The bitterness lingered on, and when Henry brought out his book there were things in it that I could not allow to pass. It was the first I knew about Henry's comments when I saw them in print. I was amazed and very upset. I have no intention of going into all the details of what was written, but it revolved to some extent around a statement in the book that on my scorecard Cooper won nine of the fifteen rounds yet I still had him losing by a quarter of a point. The facts are that I had six rounds to Bugner, five to Cooper with four even. In no round did I award a difference of more than a quarter of a point either way because it was so close all along.

Shortly after the book came out, I was a guest at the Belsize supper and was talking about it to a chap called Leslie Craymer, a solicitor who used to box for the club. He promised to read what was said in the book and very soon rang me to say that he did not like the look of it and would seek counsel's advice. A meeting was arranged and I decided to sue for libel.

'How do you feel about it?' asked Craymer when we left the meeting. I was living at Seven Kings at the time and had the house valued at £12,000. 'I've only got the house,' I told him, 'but it's paid for and I'll put it in hock if necessary.' As it turned out it never cost me a penny piece, but I would have gone all the way because my reputation and honour were at stake. They asked if I would settle out of court but Craymer said no way, we needed an apology in open court to vindicate me. The damages I agreed to accept were not large, about £1,000. I was not out to hurt Cooper, just to defend my own name.

All very sad, but Henry Cooper does not need to be bitter. He remains one of the most popular men in public life as the roar proves whenever he is introduced from the ring. He deserves it, and all I wish is that he would accept that however much he disagreed with me I was simply doing my honest best on that eventful night in 1971.

10

Trouble With the Rota

During my career as a referee I have had very few brushes with authority. One occasion was in 1970 when things came to a head to such a degree that I felt I had to make a protest about the way title contests were being allocated to referees by the Board of Control, or to be more specific by the then general secretary, Teddy Waltham.

Although I had been a 'Star' class official for a number of years, I felt I was not receiving my fair whack of the championship appointments, which are supposed to operate on a rota basis. It seemed to me, rightly or wrongly, that I was handed the difficult fights on a particular bill while another 'Star' was given a relatively straightforward title match on the same programme. I was picking up the plain fee of twelve to fifteen guineas while the other fellow had the larger fee that went with a title contest. Waltham's rota was out of true without a doubt. At the time there were five 'Star' referees but there had been fourteen British title fights since my previous appointment, and even without any deep knowledge of maths that did not add up correctly. The alternative theory to the rota being wrong was that the Board had lost confidence in me — which was my main worry I can tell you.

Just to make things worse it came to my attention that promoters, or the European Boxing Union, were ringing up from the Continent and Waltham was telling them that Harry Gibbs was unable to get time off from his job in the docks. Finally, a Royal Albert Hall tournament approached with a British bantamweight title match between Alan Rudkin and Johnny Clark top of the bill, and I received notice that I was to handle the Joe Bugner v Ray Patterson match over ten rounds. I rang Ray Clarke, the Southern Area Council secretary, and told him that I would not do the job. I told him why as well, and he replied that I was completely wrong. 'Right, well you look it up,' I told him, not angrily because we have always been good friends. 'Check the rota and see if I am out of line.'

He rang back later and confirmed that I was correct. I was ready to resign as a referee but Ray told me that was stupid. He said I should use the Board's own machinery to put the matter right, make a complaint to my Area Council, the Southern, and ask them to sort it out. In the end I took his advice and when I went before the Council I was in the room less than a minute before the chairman, David Hopkin, assured me he would represent my complaint to the Board. Not long afterwards I received a letter from the Board to the effect that my complaint against the general secretary was upheld. It was the only unfair treatment I have ever received from the Board and my reason for declining the Bugner contest was simply that, being upset, I would not have been in the right frame of mind, might have had a chip on my shoulder that could have been reflected in my actions. The reasons why I was annoyed and concerned are probably obvious. It was a matter in the first place of pride and, in the second, of money. The British title fights are the big ones and for three years I had not refereed one. I was fed up with being the bridesmaid and never the bride.

When the story came out both the managers involved, Bobby Neill for Rudkin and Dennie Mancini for Clark, as well as the promoter Mike Barrett, complained to the Board that I should have the job. Waltham's answer when the Press tackled him was that it was a Board appointment. He said that in a Cup Final the teams might want a particular referee but the appointment would still be made by the Football Association. Very true, but he ignored the fact that the Board operated a rota and that I had waited three years for an appointment. Incidentally, I was making no complaint at all about the title fight going to the Welsh referee Jim Brimmell, then recently upgraded to 'Star' class and still a colleague of mine. Only a short time after, Teddy Waltham reached sixty-five and retired, which surprised some people who had expected him to carry on for a while.

Although I missed doing that show, the Albert Hall promoter Mike Barrett came up with a consolation for me. He was co-promoter of a world featherweight title fight in Rome between the Australian Johnny Famechon, a relation of the famous French fighter Ray Famechon, and the Mexican Vincente Saldivar, and he offered me the job. Saldivar, who was trying to regain the title three years after announcing his retirement, was a remarkable champion. He fought Howard Winstone three times in epic fights, winning on points in London and Cardiff and forcing him to retire after twelve rounds at altitude in Mexico City. Howard, of course, did win the title later.

At first the Mexican and his people would not hear of a British referee for the fight, they insisted on an Italian. But in the end they accepted — and so they should have after being given those two close verdicts in Britain, not by me incidentally. The fight was a good one and Saldivar took back the title on a unanimous verdict, with me scoring for him by a wider margin than either of the Italian judges. Ironically, when it was suggested that Vincente might give Famechon a return in Australia, he intimated that he would consider it provided I was appointed as referee. As it happens the matter went no further because plans for the return fell through.

Six weeks before I refereed Muhammad Ali v Brian London at Earls Court in 1966, I handled Walter McGowan's world flyweight title match with Salvatore Burruni from Italy, as I mentioned earlier. It was a little note for the Gibbs archives that I moved from the bottom weight to the top in such a short time.

McGowan's challenge was made in the decorative setting of the Royal Albert Hall, which is a magnificent arena for boxing — although that may well infuriate lovers of classical music. The little Scot was a very complete performer and was boxing the ears off the champion when he was cut on the forehead above the right eye. The wound bled profusely but I waited for the end of that round and then went to the corner for a close look. Walter's father Joe Gans said 'There's nothing there, Harry.' Well, they all say that to referees, but the cut was not that bad. 'No, there's nothing there,' I agreed, 'you've got nothing to worry about son, box on.'

He settled down again after that and won the title on points. Afterwards I found a lot of the ringside reporters feared I was about to stop the fight because of all the blood pouring down Walter's face. But I have never been afraid of a bit of blood. The cut was away from the eye and there was no reason for me to stop the fight. McGowan said afterwards that my calm approach to his injury had helped him to win the title. I was delighted, although I did nothing I would not have done for Burruni. Another time I refereed Walter I doubt if he was as pleased because I scored him a loser to Alan Rudkin by just half a point after yet another excellent contest between two of our very best performers.

In 1966 McGowan was a busy little boy. After winning the world flyweight title in June he outpointed Rudkin in London to become British bantamweight champion. A referee from the Midlands gave him the verdict and then Rudkin had to wait nearly two years before he was given a second chance, this time at the Belle Vue arena in Manchester.

This was a great deal nearer the blond headed little Rudkin's home city of Liverpool and the Scouse brigade were out in force. They saw their bustling hero start well but then face a tremendous assault from the Scot. They were a great-hearted pair and at the end I made it 73½ to 73, a difference of two rounds by the scoring in force then.

The late George Whiting of the London Evening Standard, one of the great boxing writers with a fascinating turn of phrase, agreed that Rudkin had the edge, a razor edge, and summed up 'Great winner . . . great loser . . . great fight.'

Still jumping around the weights, I must mention a fighter I cannot recall ever refereeing but who was pound for pound one of the great British boxers — Dave Charnley. I took Dave abroad on representive duty as an amateur and I saw his second attempt on the world lightweight title. He lost to Joe Brown in Houston, Texas, where he was injured and forced to retire in five rounds, but he was then given a return in London. It was definitely close and I thought Charnley had done enough, but the man in charge, Tommy Little, did not agree unfortunately. Dave reigned supreme in Britain and Europe in the early sixties and even took on welterweights with success. I always rated Peter Waterman but he was well beaten when he met Charnley in a catch-weights match.

John Stracey's great performance when he went all the way to Mexico City to lift the world welterweight title from José Napoles set British boxing alight. It was in December 1975 that John H. defied altitude and Napoles's home advantage to become champion, and it gave particular satisfaction to those of us in boxing who had watched the lad from Bethnal Green build up his career. I had refereed John often, of course, on the way up, battling his way through with his brow puckered in that familiar frown of concentration.

In those days the British Board was still able to stand by its principles and insist that even world title contests here followed our rule of one referee and no judges. Eventually Britain was forced to toe the line and agree to judges sharing the decision in world fights here. I was against the move to two judges and a referee. Now the World Boxing Council have gone a step further and voted for three judges and a referee who handles the contest but does not have a say in the verdict. The strongest comment I dare offer here is 'rubbish'!

In his first defence Stracey gave British boxing yet another tonic because he was superb at Wembley against the snappy American Hedgemon Lewis. After such a triumph overseas, his defence at Wembley was built up as a great occasion and Terry Lawless, then Stracey's manager, made sure that his Cockney boy was right on top of his form, very sharp and powerful. As usual I kept the initial instructions brief in the ring and as I sent them back to their corners John fixed Hedgemon with a steely glare and told him 'This is for real Hedgemon.' That was all that was said but I feel it had a lot to do with Lewis coming out so fast and getting stuck in straight away. For a few rounds Stracey was not in it, not outclassed of course but having to weather the American's skilful storm. Then Lewis began to lose momentum and finally blew up. Those spindly legs of his began to go and John stopped him in style. When Stracey had a man in trouble he never left him, he was a fine winning fighter.

John lost his world crown to the talented American Carlos Palomino — who later returned to Wembley to land a perfect knock-out left hook to ruin the challenge of the ferocious Fen Tiger, Dave 'Boy' Green, just as Green was edging ahead. After Stracey's defeat the match the British crowds wanted to see was Stracey v Green and when the money was put up and the contracts signed Wembley was packed to the rafters. There was no title at stake but the contest was made by public demand. Stracey's Bethnal Green mob were out in force, half the East End in fact, and so were those wonderful followers from the Fens who have brought so much fun and enthusiasm to Green's career.

The fight itself was a rugged one and I issued a number of warnings to both men for the way they were careless with their heads. As early as the first round I had occasion to wag a finger at Green and warn him about his head, but in the second I felt John overplayed it when he showed out to me because David's head was nowhere near that time. Of course it was in the vicinity, but that was inevitable in a close-quarter battle. When a bloke nuts deliberately, that is intending to damage, he does it quickly and it is as sharp as a punch. There is no holding your chin up and trying to impress a referee you are being nutted because by then you have been really hurt if the deed has been done by an expert. Later in the same contest I warned Stracey for being careless with his head, too.

All round it was a clash of styles, but Green's famous muck-spreader punch, a sweeping right swing, kept landing on the same place near John's left eye and, of course, it puffed up. Stracey had a terrific seventh round and the two fighters were talking in the clinches. I heard Green ask 'Is that the hardest you can hit?' A round or two later I pulled Stracey out because he was taking a bit of a hiding. I would say that in that fight Green was at the peak of his career, certainly I have never seen him in form like it since.

One of the boxing greats I remember vividly, even though I refereed him only once, was Sugar Ray Robinson. He was no stranger to Britain of course, and in 1951, six years before I turned to refereeing, he was part of a sensation when he lost his world middleweight title to Randolph Turpin at Harringay Arena. When I gained the honour of entering the ring with this fine champion he was making his last appearance in Britain, meeting a willing Nigerian named Johnny Angel. After six rounds I had seen enough and stopped it. Robinson was skating it and I felt Angel had taken sufficient punishment. Some of the customers at the Anglo-American Sporting Club did not agree and started slow handclapping and thumping the tables. Reg Gutteridge, boxing writer from the old Evening News and ITV commentator, asked me 'What do you think of that Harry?'

I replied that I was not there to give the crowd a Roman Holiday, I was appointed to look after Angel and the other guy, who just happened to be Sugar Ray Robinson. Angel had not been on the floor but I saw no point in the contest continuing any further. I was not bothered about the crowd's bad manners, only about what was right for both boxers. Robinson's only comment in the ring was 'Quite right, ref.' He did not wish to hurt any opponent unnecessarily I am sure, which is rather like Larry Holmes's attitude against Muhammad Ali when it seemed to me, from a distance of course, that he was not punching his weight because he did not want to hurt Ali. Robinson was a brilliant performer and I have enjoyed meeting him on a number of occasions since.

Still with middleweights — a weight which I feel has produced many of the great contests — and I come to Mark Rowe, the blond pig farmer from Kent. I am not claiming that Mark was the greatest, but for strength and courage he took a lot of beating. He could whack, too, and was a tremendous body puncher, but, sadly, took too much himself. Mark is such a pleasant fellow that I have seen him get opponents in trouble and walk away. I shall always remember the way his fight with Pat Dwyer was built up; I think there was a Rolls Royce resting on it as a side stake. Dwyer, a bouncy sort of fighter from Liverpool, was very much the vogue for a while with one group of well-breeched fight followers, and, after all the pre-fight publicity, he went in and stopped Mark.

Rowe finally won the title in 1970 by stopping another Liverpool boy, Les McAteer, in fourteen rounds at Wembley. Mark soaked up punishment early on but kept padding forward until McAteer was completely exhausted and was stopped in the fourteenth. Only four months later Rowe was stopped at Wembley by Bunny Sterling and he did not have another chance at the British title until April 1973 when he was given a return with Sterling, again at Wembley and this time with me in charge.

In the meantime Sterling had proved himself a very good champion, an artful boxer and damaging hitter. He proved too smart for Rowe once again, only this time it went the full fifteen rounds before I gave it to Sterling by 74 points to 73 — and remember we were still using the quarter-point margins then. A few of Rowe's supporters booed, but most people agreed it was about right. Sterling's manager George Francis, a man I first knew in the docks who coached the St Pancras amateur club after I left, made a comment to Boxing News that I appreciated. George said: 'As far as I'm concerned Harry Gibbs is the best referee in Europe and perhaps in the world, and if he saw it as Bunny winning by a point that's good enough for me.'

Terry Downes, of course, is another middleweight of my era who stands out. I can only recall actually refereeing him once although I watched him fight on many occasions. Terry was a real 'good 'un', a tearaway and very brave. He looks well now, I am glad to say and sounds all right for certain because I hear him often enough, shouting at me while I am in the ring working. That Cockney gravel voice grinds out from a few rows back 'Now then, Harry Gibbs, watch him holding.' He is always having a go at me, but I like the fellow and he was great for the game.

11

A Gathering of Champions

Alan Minter, John Conteh, Maurice Hope, Jim Watt and the Finnegans — what an array of champions and what a cluster of refereeing memories they have given me over the years!

Minter first. Continuing the line of crowd-pleasing middleweights, he is a young man who has kept battling in the face of all sorts of problems, all the way through to that wonderful night when he won the world title in Las Vegas. It was a great achievement to take a title on foreign soil and it made him the only undisputed champion of the lot, recognised by both the World Boxing Council and their great rivals the World Boxing Association.

When Minter was just a bright young amateur prospect from Crawley he went to the 1972 Olympics in Munich and was robbed against a West German. It was very bad luck because he seemed to beat the German by a mile. As a pro he did his utmost to live up to his 'Boom-Boom' nickname with plenty of crash-bang performances, but hit a bad spell when a series of cuts threatened his career. He came through that dodgy patch in the end and lost the 'Boom-Boom' image once his manager Doug Bidwell, who is also his father-in-law, brought in the former British featherweight champion Bobby Neill as his technical adviser. After that Alan developed as a superb box-fighter winning British, European and world titles in succession.

It was during Alan's problem spell that I refereed him at the Royal Albert Hall against a boy called Jan Magdiarz who boxed out of Southampton. This was before Alan had collected any pro titles and evidently they had met before, in fact several times. On the previous two occasions Minter lost on cut eyes. A lot of fighters have a bogeyman as Warnock was to Benny Lynch, and evidently Magdiarz was the same to Minter.

From the start I was in a quandary because they would not go near each other. I went backwards and forwards to the corners, talking to them and their managers, three times each I believe. During the rounds I was doing my usual exhortation bit, but the customers were becoming decidedly restive and making their feelings known with a slow handclap. Finally they began to throw things, including several meat pies. One fell into the ring close to me and did not burst out of its wrapping, so I picked it up and added some badly-needed light relief to the proceedings by handing it to someone at the ringside and telling him to hang on to it for my break the next morning.

I carried on doing my utmost to persuade them to have a fight but finally I had had enough and turned the pair of them out. I was sorry to do it because I have always felt Minter has been a credit to the game all through. They were hauled up before the Board of Control and fined £500 each. I feel that both managers realised there was not a lot else I could have done, and while we were at the Board's offices for the hearing Magdiarz's manager Jack Bishop was saying he knew his man had to be punished. Whatever the reasons, they were both professional men with real ability who on that particular night were not doing their jobs.

Once Minter threw off his injury worries his career took off again and he has figured in a host of good fights, including those three magnificent British title battles against Kevin Finnegan.

For a period during Alan's career I did not handle his contests, which was a wise and deliberate move by the Board of Control because I had gone to law after reading comments in a local newspaper purported to have been made by Doug Bidwell. They did not refer to one of Alan's contests but I was relieved not to referee him at that time because it would have put me under strain. The boxer involved was Alan's brother Mickey. I refereed him at Southend and in my view he was narrowly defeated. Soon afterwards I refereed him again, this time at Manor Place Baths in Walworth, and once more he was beaten. It was a close fight but on each occasion the decision was well received by the majority of the crowd.

At Manor Place Bidwell spoke to me in the ring after the fight and implied that I had something against the Minters. I came back at him fast: 'What do you mean? Who are you talking to?' upon which he took the remark back and asked me to accept his apology, which I did. When I got out, the Area representative Bill Sheeran asked me what was said but I told him the matter was closed and no further action was necessary. However, a couple of weeks later a bloke handed me a copy of Bidwell's local paper that included quotes from Bidwell which I did not like at all. I showed the paper to my solicitor and he went to work. I received a public apology and agreed damages, and the case was settled out of court.

Since then I have got along well enough with Bidwell and very well with Alan. I have handled contests involving Bidwell's fighters since and as far as I am concerned the incident is over and forgotten. But as a pro referee I do not feel I can afford to ignore a slur on my character. Shakespeare sums it up well in Richard II:

> The purest treasure mortal times afford
> Is spotless reputation; that away
> Men are but gilded loam or painted clay.
> A jewel in a ten-times barred-up chest
> Is a bold spirit in a loyal breast.
> Mine honour is my life; both grow in one,
> Take honour from me, and my life is done.

No, I did not reel that off without looking it up, but I did have the crucial bits in my head. I do react strongly to suggestions that I make any kind of fortune out of boxing and I have a very obvious answer to them. I work on shifts at a dock container base, often I am at work before 7 am. I have a little house and a little car. If I were bent or making money hand-over-fist, I would have a Daimler and a place on Hampstead Heath.

Minter was made to wait a very long time for his world title chance, but finally Vito Antuofermo had to meet him in Las Vegas. Minter won on points and then came back home to Wembley for the return. It was one of those nights with real atmosphere and Minter was brilliant: he picked Antuofermo off, cut him and stopped him.

Next came another home clash, this time against Marvin Hagler from Boston, Massachusetts. It was a late-night start at Wembley to fit in with American television, the source of big money in boxing these days. I went along anticipating one heck of a scrap after having a preview of Hagler in action during one of my trips to Las Vegas. I was there in fact to judge the world welterweight match between Wilfredo Benitez and Sugar Ray Leonard and on the same bill Antuofermo was making a middleweight defence against Hagler. The black man from Boston is a shaven-headed, ferocious-looking character — as the British public discovered when he came to Wembley — and he gave Antuofermo a real fright. In fact, despite the champion's gameness I thought Hagler won comfortably and was surprised when they called it a draw.

For the Minter-Hagler match I had a seat just behind Minter's corner, expectant and wary on Alan's behalf. I hoped he would show the controlled power he had against Antuofermo in their second meeting but, sadly, he was much too wild despite all the instructions from his corner to concentrate on his boxing. From my seat I heard clearly when manager Bidwell told Alan in no uncertain terms to go out there and box. These orders were repeated before the second round, but then Minter caught Hagler a good punch, realised he had staggered him and rushed in for the kill. It was much too early. Hagler's legs went sure enough, but early in a fight men who are as superbly fit as this pair recover so quickly.

Before long, in the third round in fact, it was Alan who was stopped and then the trouble started from the crowd, up on the balconies mainly. Hagler won fair and square and, to my sorrow, we lost our reputation for giving visiting fighters a square deal whatever the circumstances. Hagler did not receive his just desserts. He was not acclaimed from the ring as a worthy champion as he should have been, and as so many other foreign fighters have been in British rings in the past. When the cans and plastic bottles rained down I moved along to stand in front of the wife of the American promoter Bob Arum to shield her and, luckily, it was soon over. It was a rare event in British boxing and left a sour taste. I know it upset Alan too. He never claimed Hagler stepped out of line in any way, nutted him or did anything wrong; he gave his supporters a good example, but just a few did not follow it.

Naturally the whole thing received great publicity and all kinds of theories were put forward about the causes of the trouble. In my opinion it was simply drink talking, dictating the actions of a disappointed few. I doubt if the patriotic atmosphere built up in the big fight preliminaries had much to do with it, it never has before that I can recall. The crowd as a whole were none too happy. They had paid a considerable amount of money to see a poor supporting bill and then their hero was done inside a few rounds. Half of them further back were suspicious that Hagler's head had gone in to do the damage, which, of course, it had not.

While Minter reigned as middleweight king, Scotland's Jim Watt ruled as the World Boxing Council's lightweight champion and Maurice Hope, surely one of the most gallant of our fighters, proudly retained his WBC light-middleweight title. Three world champions all at the same time was great for British boxing, particularly with such a fine trio of sportsmen carrying the banner for us.

Maurice, a product of the famous Repton Club who have produced so many champions from the Bethnal Green area, came to Britain from Antigua when he was young. I have followed his boxing career with interest and pleasure and have no hesitation in naming him one of my favourite fighters. Pure grit is the best way to describe Mo's approach to life. He endured injuries, frustrations and setbacks to emerge as a remarkable champion. Even when his career was threatened by an eye injury he retained his dignity.

I refereed Mo on several occasions on his way to the top and was a judge in Berlin the night he challenged Eckhard Dagge for the world title. I scored him a clear winner, but the result was a draw and he waited another four years before being given a second chance. When it came he won handsomely inside the distance, making scoring superfluous. Maurice and I have a standing joke going back to the night I lent him a white towel at an out-of-town show he was appearing in. I never got it back and now whenever we meet I ask him for it. I have had some hilarious replies from him.

I think the best quality Mo has is his grim determination; he is prepared to force himself beyond the point of no return if necessary. I have read where he has stated at a Press conference that he is prepared to drive himself to any lengths to keep his title. Many champions have said that but only Mo means it. He has character and pride and has impressed me more than just about any champion I have met.

Jim Watt runs Mo very close because this dapper Scot is another of the sport's gentlemen. Incidentally, if you think I am simply handing out bouquets, think again. I am sure that the vast majority of people in sport would agree with me one hundred per cent. Watt stands out as a fine champion — feet on the ground, and success has not increased his hat size in the slightest. Mind you, I am biased in favour of Scots. When I was a kid of nineteen and slung into a German prison camp I found myself with a whole crowd of Scots. They were old soldiers, mostly with service in India, and they took care of me, kept my morale up. Hard people but great.

Over the years I have refereed Watt from time to time, but my best memories of him are in world title fights in Glasgow, the city where he rules as King of Boxing. The night he won the title by stopping Alfredo Pitalua from Colombia I was seated by the ring as a judge, pressed into service because a judge from abroad had not arrived. Jim did not wait for voting time, he stopped Pitalua in style and the Kelvin Hall erupted. In the middle of the crush a Scotsman all done up in his tartan tapped me on the shoulder. I brushed him off. After all I was wearing a dinner suit, C & A special, and did not want it damaged. In fact all he was after was to offer me a drink and I took a swig out of his Scotch bottle. Those Scots always go prepared!

I was judging again when Jim met Sean O'Grady in the smaller Kelvin Arena and despite a cut he came through once more to stop his man. Did he butt his opponent? In my view he did not. There was an accidental clash of heads and the fight had to be stopped in the end, not from the cut itself but because O'Grady's corner people failed to stop the bleeding. The way they went about it, sloshing so much water around, they had little chance.

Of all Britain's world champions of the past decade light heavyweight John Conteh, the handsome lad from Liverpool, must rate as the most controversial. I am not concerned with John's rows outside the ring, his brushes with authority of various kinds and the publicity that has followed him around, but only with his fighting performances.

As he swept onto the title scene, learning his trade along the way, I refereed him and was impressed with his talent. Then I was handed the refereeing job when he fought for the World Boxing Council's title at Wembley against a strong, stubborn Argentinian called Jorge Ahumada. This was Conteh at his best and there was no way Ahumada was going to upset him that night, although I had to take Conteh to task myself in the last round. He went in with the head and I put my hand there to slow him up. He nodded at the warning and went back to work, just to make certain. It was a thrilling night and the huge crowd appreciated it to the full. Afterwards I received a letter I will always treasure, from the Board's president Mr J. Onslow Fane, which said that he had seen a world champion boxer and a world champion referee.

Conteh ran into various problems as world champion until he was finally stripped of the title. When he began to fight again I remember refereeing him at the Anglo-American Sporting Club in a warm-up fight and giving a draw, a rare event for me as I have mentioned before. He met the American Jesse Burnett, an awkward character with plenty of experience and a useful, sneaky punch. He sent Conteh over right on the bell at the end of the first round and I have to admit I did not see the punch at all. I thought John had slipped and it was only when I pulled him up and started to lead him to his corner that I noticed his definite stagger.

'Hello' I thought, 'he must have been chinned.' Conteh recovered quickly, pecked away with his left jab and Burnett did not press home his advantage, although he did put John in trouble again later. One newspaperman took me to task for not giving Conteh the decision because he scored more clean blows while others thought the American won. I simply did not believe John deserved it. I was very disappointed in him and for him that night. As for Burnett, he and his manager were delighted with the draw.

Conteh was given a chance to regain the world title when he met Matt Franklin, now calling himself Matthew Saad Muhammad, in Atlantic City, New Jersey, and I was there as one of the judges. That was in 1979 and the next year I was back again for the return. Both fights went to Franklin but there was a vast difference between them, indeed John went close to winning the first time and I had him in front by one point going into the thirteenth. He boxed beautifully up to then, but once he was floored he went to pieces in the last two rounds and the champion just took a unanimous decision.

The return was held in the theatre at the Resorts International Hotel and Casino, again in Atlantic City. They tell me Conteh looked magnificent in training, but sadly he never showed any of it in the ring. Franklin, or Saad Muhammad, started as he finished the first time and the British boy was never in it. If Conteh had boxed as he did in the earlier fight he might have had a chance, but as soon as he stepped into that ring he did not seem right to me. He caught a few hard punches but simply was not in business at all that night. Afterwards, I am told because I saw nothing of it, he went on a spree and finished up causing a bit of a rumpus around the hotel early next morning.

Now for the Finnegans — Chris and Kevin, two of the greatest characters I have had the pleasure to referee. Chris was first on the pro scene after winning his Olympic Gold medal. There were those who said he was too much the amateur and would not make a top professional — what a joke! The Finnegans were real professionals and a credit to the game. Chris is a great personality. He does not have a mean bone in his body so far as taking advantage of a referee is concerned and I never heard him scream or even moan about a decision. After one of his title fights with Conteh there was considerable talk about the head going in, but Chris made no complaint.

When Chris met Bob Foster for the world title at Wembley in 1972 he lost in the fourteenth round. I was not in charge, but I was three years later when he and Gypsy Johnny Frankham met at the Royal Albert Hall for the British title, at that stage left vacant by Conteh. It was a thrilling battle, just like their return five months later. The place was packed with intensely partisan followers as two wonderful characters sorted it out in the ring, with me keeping a cautious eye. Gypsy John simply kidded Chris out of it that night; he was a cheeky devil and he kept grinning and turning on all his tricks.

Chris was badly cut near one eye and at the end it was desperately close. I felt Frankham was home by a quarter of a point and the place was red hot as I raised his hand. If ever the ingredients were there for a riot that was it — Finnegan could have set the place alight but he took it like a gentleman. Afterwards I believe there was a punch-up backstage between the two families that never went to purse offers. But next day, Derby Day, both boys were together on the course at Epsom, full of a lot more spirit than just sportsmanship I am sure.

After the fight the worst slating I received came from Chris's missus, Cheryl, but then I have known her give other referees a far worse seeing to. We've all been through the hook from Cheryl when she has been aggrieved, but she was always heart and soul in support of her man.

Although Kevin never fought for a world title I reckon he was just as good as Chris — maybe in some ways a bit better — and his courage was remarkable, as I discovered the night he met the West German Frank Reiche at Wembley. Kevin was European champion at the time and this was just a fill-in for him. He built up an early lead and seemed to be going well, only what I did not know was that Reiche had broken Kevin's jaw. Kev covered it up from me and I only tumbled it in the last round when he was hit flush on the chin. It was like an animal's cry of pain as he grunted and I realised something was seriously wrong. Before that he had used all his skill to duck inside and get through, which he was able to do because he was such a clever boxer. When at last he cried out it was right on the bell and when I walked to his corner his trainer, Freddie Hill, said 'He's got a broken jaw, Harry.' I felt like kicking him just at that moment because I would have stopped the fight had I realised the damage. Kevin won the contest but he could have been hurt far more seriously than he was.

When the jaw had mended the European Boxing Union refused to allow Kevin a warm-up fight and he lost the title to Gratien Tonna, the bully of a Frenchman Minter later beat so convincingly. It always rankled with Finnegan and right at the end of his career he went to Paris to meet Tonna again and gave a glorious performance to take back the title. Kevin is the man who visited Paris earlier in his career to take the European title from local hero Jean-Claude Bouttier, and who went to Boston twice for heroic battles with Hagler before being cut.

I will never forget the night the Old Fox took back the British title by outsmarting young Tony Sibson from Leicester: he surprised everyone and outmanoeuvred him all the way. Poor Sibson seemed mesmerised as the maestro darted in and out stealing the points early on, something I appreciated more than anyone, being right in there with them. If you want to know about courage in the ring — raspberry we Cockneys call it — then look no further than the Finnegans. They never knew when they were beat.

Another man of outstanding character is Ken Buchanan, the Scot from Edinburgh, who was lightweight champion of Britain, Europe and the world. I mention Buchanan here just so you know I have not forgotten him, but I will write in more detail about him in my chapter on fights abroad. Strangely, Ken was starved of big-money fights here in Britain and gave many of his finest performances away from home.

Moving back to the middleweights, I always admired Wally Swift and it was a knife-edge occasion when, right at the end of his career, he defended the British title at Nottingham Ice Rink against young Johnny Pritchett. It was very much a domestic affair: Swift came from Nottingham itself, Pritchett from the village of Bingham just outside and the place was packed. It turned out to be a gripping fight, one of the good ones to handle even though it was close.

Swift was cut near the left eye about the seventh round and I finally had to stop it in the twelfth. At that stage Pritchett was slightly in front and I felt Wally could not see out of the left eye any longer. The crowd went mad, although not with rage I am happy to recall, and Swift and his manager George Biddles took it well. Pritchett was undefeated as British champion and then went to Italy to challenge Juan-Carlos Duran in Milan, only to be disqualified which was a most strange verdict as John was in front. He retired to concentrate on his business interest and now serves on the Southern Area Council of the Board.

A featherweight champion I will always remember was Evan Armstrong from Ayr, a stringy Scot with tremendous determination and ability. I can see him now, a proper clansman. I used to imagine him roaring down from the Highlands in the old days brandishing his claymore. When he met another Scot, Vernon Sollas, in a non-title match at the Royal Albert Hall Evan took plenty of stick early on from a snappy little mover who had his eyes very much on a title chance. But Evan had a very deceptive strength and was biding his time. Danny Vary, his trainer, told me that after the seventh round he told them in the corner: 'He's done his quickstep, his dancing, now it's my turn.' Out he went for the eighth and Sollas was knocked out before it ended.

Against Allan Richardson in a British and Commonwealth title defence in 1974 Evan was cut badly in the early rounds but still pulled it out. Richardson, a gritty little Yorkshireman, made it a terrific battle and yet simply had to wilt in the end and was stopped in the eleventh.

The smaller men may not attract the huge purses the bigger fellows receive but they have given us a great many epic contests to savour and I have been fortunate to referee men like Rudkin and McGowan, and Johnny Clark, Dave Needham and Paddy Maguire.

Clark failed twice in great fights with Rudkin and then took the bantamweight title against Paddy Maguire when Rudkin retired. Clark relinquished the title and Maguire tried again, this time at Nottingham Ice Rink against local favourite Dave Needham, the former Commonwealth Games amateur champion. Maguire fought his heart out but Needham was the master in a thrilling match between a couple of gamecocks who never gave up. Afterwards Maguire's wife, loyal to the last, took me to task a little, but there was no doubt in my mind and some ringsiders scored it to Needham by even more. Still, Maguire had another go and took the title from Needham when he beat him in fourteen rounds at the World Sporting Club in London nearly a year later.

So many fighters have genuine courage that I would not presume to put them in any kind of order, but Harry Scott, the rugged electrician from Bootle, qualified for a medal the night he took on American Rubin Carter at the Albert Hall. Carter was one of the most feared men of his day, and I believe he is still in prison in America for murder. He was a frightening sight with his shaven head and mandarin moustache, and he could fight too. Only on this night Scott traded him pretty well blow for blow, lasting nine rounds before I stopped it because he was badly cut near the left eye. It caused a row, of course, but I had not made a hasty decision because I gave Scott plenty of chance to work before stepping in. In any case I had Carter in front at the time. Whatever the result, though, the glory went to Scott one hundred per cent. They met again and Scott won on points. I was not scoring but I did not feel he made it.

The final words in this chapter I leave for another of Britain's bravest warriors, Johnny Owen, who was indeed one of the most gallant men I have watched and refereed. When Owen died in Los Angeles following his world bantam-weight title challenge to Lupe Pintor, it was one of the great disasters in boxing and, of course, a deep personal tragedy for all who knew the matchstick-thin Welsh boy. More than virtually any other fighter Owen had lived for boxing. It gave him his identity and in the ring or even in the gym, the shy lad from Merthyr became a man of immense stature.

I was privileged to referee Johnny's last fight in Britain when he defended the British and Commonwealth titles against John Feeney from Hartlepool at Wembley. Owen held the European title, too, but it was not on the line that night. Feeney is a talented boy, but Owen drove forward from the start. He had something of the quality another great Welshman little Jimmy Wilde must have had and in the fifteenth round was marching on with just as much strength to finish a clear winner. I was most impressed with his fitness, his skill and his sportsmanship. His death stunned me, along with everyone else in boxing, but his memory is a glorious one because he was a shining example of all that is best in the sport.

12

You Have to Be the Guv'nor

I believe it was King Henry V who said 'Now the game's afoot' before some major battle, and I think of that line when I stand in a boxing ring giving final brief instructions to a pair of superb athletes. If I put a hand on each, very often I would be able to feel them trembling like finely-trained greyhounds nervous in the trap or whippets ready to be slipped. They are eager to start, straining at the leash to get into the fray. Nine times out of ten they are completely fit men and I think to myself that they have every right to be more on edge than I am because soon they will have to do the giving and the taking, while I stand only in judgment. That does not mean that I am a stranger to nerves. I may not be as tense now as when I started refereeing, or as I was in my first few major contests, but I still find my stomach tightening as fight-time approaches.

I like to arrive at a hall well ahead of the tournament, settle down and make sure everything is in order. Then, two or three minutes before I am due to step into the ring, I feel the tenseness coming on. I may not want to go for a pee so often now, but I am glad to be nervous, on edge to a certain degree, because I owe it to the fighters to be on my toes and make no mistake. The first duty of a referee is to the boxers themselves, their safety should be his first consideration. The word safety may seem odd but I do mean safety. The referee who has complete control, who knows exactly when to step in, precisely the moment when a boxer is in trouble and has no more to give, is the man doing the job correctly. Scoring is vital of course, but only combined with safety.

I once watched a kid in a preliminary fight, only a six-rounder, take a terrible hiding. It was clear after two or three rounds that he was outclassed but the referee could not see it and the corner, apparently, couldn't either. Finally the other bloke crashed in a right, down went the poor little blighter, cracked the back of his head on the canvas and was carried out on a stretcher. That is a terrible sight and it was so unnecessary in this case. When a fighter has done his best, given value for money, he should be rescued at the right time — and I am not saying for a moment that all of us get it exactly right every time. If a referee can do that he leaves the loser eager to try again, possibly aggrieved with the ref but with his spirit intact. When the referee acts too late a boxer may well be lost to the sport, even if he escapes serious injury.

In the ring I call the two lads together and I always keep to the same words for the short talk-in before the start. They were taught me by Ray Clarke, the Board general secretary, when I was starting and they run: 'You are boxing under the British Boxing Board of Control rules. Always punch with the knuckle part of the glove and when I tell you to break, break, I insist on that. If one man goes down, the other goes to a neutral corner and stays there until I give the order to box on, and above all, defend yourselves at all times.' That is it, finish. I do not like any of that stuff the Americans seem to dish up about having a good clean fight. These lads are professionals and should know their jobs.

Once a contest has started a good referee should not be seen. He has to be heard by the boxers but you try not to keep calling out 'break' all the time. You interject words of encouragement like 'Come on, work' or 'Let's see you work, lads', and when they do you say 'Well done, son.' The public does not really hear you, but the boxers do. The idea is to gain their confidence, and my aim in doing that is to draw their best work from them, in their interests and those of the paying customers because this is after all an entertainment as well as a sport. If you can help two men to work really well, say over ten rounds, it makes for great entertainment. My idea of boxing is to see two men well matched, as equal as possible, and then to find out who will prevail. It is a fascinating thing and that is why I am always looking for a winner in every round, let alone every contest. I know I have written that before but it is important.

When I go back to my corner between rounds I have about half a minute to mark my card after quickly weighing up the previous round. I am not looking simply at the quantity of punches landed on the target area, but at the quality as well. It is impossible to count the number of blows struck by each man so you have to consider everything and allow your brain, aided by experience, to programme out who won the round. Then, once the card is marked, a referee must make sure that all is well in each corner, walk over to examine any wound that might be serious, take a careful look at a man who has been floored in the previous round or administer a quiet warning if necessary.

A referee, whatever he feels inside, should appear to be completely in charge at all times, as expressionless as possible. But he must never appear a bully; officiousness is a vice in a referee because men always react better to a quiet warning, even when it is direct and very much to the point.

Old Barry Dalby was one who always looked as if he was very much the guv'nor, and when I joined the refereeing ranks there were men around like Jack Hart, Ike Powell and Tommy Little who had been years in the game. Talking to them, watching them and working alongside them helped considerably. Some of their knowledge must have rubbed off and I will always recall Jack telling me: 'Harry, an honest decision is a good decision, don't ever forget that.' I took that to mean that even when a referee erred, as long as he had made an honest mistake the decision must be a good one, at least for his own peace of mind. That is the way I see it, although I still ponder over the close ones. A decision is a matter of opinion and I respect other views, only I am the man who is being paid to go out on a limb, and not simply say over a beer afterwards: 'I scored so-and-so the winner.'

To a referee the boxers should become, as far as possible, just two pairs of different coloured shorts. When I climb through the ropes I try to put names and reputations out of my mind — it does not matter that one man is a champion. In America they say a challenger has to do something special to take the title away from a reigning champion but that is a fallacy here. Both men start equal under British rules and if it is close the decision is just as likely to go to the challenger as to the champion.

Although the ringside customers may have a good view, always remember the referee is closest to the action and is therefore the man in the best position to know exactly what is going on. From further back than two or three rows it is difficult to judge the merit of punches and the further back you go the harder it is.

In long contests spectators, caught up in the action as it happens, often forget what has gone on in the early rounds, but the referee can never forget. His impression of those rounds is down, indelibly, on his scorecard. The Board of Control has devised a scorecard that must be completed as each round ends. Whatever the referee puts on the card goes through onto the carbon copy and it is impossible to cheat. If a referee makes a mistake he has to correct it immediately, during the contest, by going to the steward in charge or a Board inspector to have the alteration initialled. He cannot wait until the fight ends. I can only remember one occasion when I faced this embarrassment.

As a referee you have to develop your own style and try

to appear the coolest man in the hall. When you are handling an exciting and even contest the crowd becomes deeply involved. Even the neutrals are carried away with the suspense and the drama, but one man has to keep his head completely — the referee. He has to be detached and put anything shouted out from the audience out of his mind. That is not always easy, indeed sometimes it is impossible. You get used to reminders to 'Do your flies up, ref' so you are unlikely to catch me looking down for that one, but I remember once being forced to a grin at Shoreditch Town Hall while I was working as a labour master at Aberdeen Wharf. It was in the days when an hour of day-work in the docks brought in 3s 6d, which was a reasonable sum then. I was marking my card in the corner between rounds when someone shouted out 'Put him down for another hour's day-work, Harry.' That brought a roar of laughter from the many dockers there. As I say you try to ignore it but you cannot help a grin now and again — after all it is a sport and what is life without a laugh or two.

The docks, prison-camp life and my own boxing and training experiences have all gone into building up my approach to refereeing. All those events, varied and hectic at times, must have given me an insight into controlling men. This is what I have done ever since the war — the docks are a man's world apart from the offices — and I am sure it has helped me in the ring.

There is always a good side to any bloke. You learn that in the docks and apply it too. With boxers it is the same: you must treat them as human beings but you must be firm. Boxers respect that, generally anyway. In all walks of life there are occasions when an act of kindness is taken as an act of weakness, and it is the same in the ring. You have to watch that because if you are a weak referee they will soon find you out. After all, they are professionals and if they can get an easy job they will. You watch for the times when a man feigns a low blow to try to get a disqualification — and a lot of the boys are fine actors when they want to be. I try to nip in quick, pull a boy up, talk to him and keep him going.

As you work there is always plenty of comment coming from the boxers' corners, although not nearly so much in Britain as abroad. The British rule is for strict silence from the cornermen and Board inspectors are on hand to enforce it. Of course, they do not manage it all the time and a referee has the power to order a man out of a corner if he should get carried away completely. He would tell the inspector that he was ordering so-and-so out of the corner and to make sure he stayed away from it for the rest of the fight. It does not happen often but you would be surprised how some of them become really wound up. I cannot see that it helps their fighters at all.

In the States they go screaming mad sometimes, it is terrible but I doubt very much if the boxers themselves absorb more than a tiny fraction of the instructions yelled out to them. I would not mind a pound for every time I have heard someone shout out 'Be first, be first', and as that is what every fighter is trying to be anyway it really is meaningless. Naturally there *are* times when a professional cornerman on his toes can convey clear instructions to his boxer. The best illustration is when a man goes down and turns to look at his corner, then he is told by simple, clear gestures how long to stay down and when to rise. But that ring is a lonely place. A second can indicate something but only the fighter is in there to do anything about it. A boxer's reaction to his corner when he is knocked down can, in fact, be of assistance to a referee because it gives him an indication of how badly hurt the man is. If he leaps up quickly it often means that he is dazed, his wits scattered. But if, as a good pro should, he gets up onto one knee, looks to his corner and rises at seven or eight in good time to box on, you know he is still very much in the contest.

Allowing for natural bias I am convinced that the British system of having just one man — the referee — to control and decide a contest is the best. Certainly it is here because our standards are high and consequently our referees are in demand abroad because people know our fairness and our integrity are better than just about anywhere else. In my view having two judges does not bring an improvement or provide better decisions. Now the World Boxing Council has voted to have three judges to decide and a non-voting referee to control world title fights, and that is simply stupid. Not so long ago I went to the Far East to referee a world flyweight title fight between a Japanese and a South Korean. Each had a judge from his own country and each judge voted for his own man. I am sure that bias, unconscious bias, came into it and they certainly did not see the fighters just as two pairs of shorts.

After the contest the crowd does not remember judges, only the referee and it is he who has to take the rap. Our system has stood up over the years and world champions were always content to defend in Britain with just one British referee to give the decision. There have been many instances of decisions going to overseas boxers, and close, controversial decisions too. Tommy Little went against Dave Charnley by an extremely narrow margin when he challenged Joe Brown for the world lightweight title in London, and Vincente Saldivar was twice given close verdicts in Britain when he defended the world featherweight title against Howard Winstone. In the case of the Charnley fight I was told that Brown's manager commented: 'What a fool the referee was. I wish he had given it to Charnley because it would have made a great return.' Needless to say, I do not agree. Tommy was right: he called it exactly as he saw it.

One thing that amazes me about refereeing generally is the number of drawn rounds that are revealed when the scores are announced, even in world title fights. It seems that so many referees and judges sit on the fence, which makes nonsense of what I have said about trying to find a winner in every round if possible. It is no good trying to hedge your bets, the rounds must be scored on merit right from the first bell.

In Britain today we score each round out of ten marks, descending in halves. The man who wins the round is given ten, the loser a lesser score, usually 10-9½ unless the margin between the men in that particular round is wide. Naturally a drawn round is scored 10-10. Now, 10-9½ decides the round but simply to write that down on the card automatically is wrong. How about the man who wins a round decisively? He is entitled to the other half point to win 10-9. I am always prepared to make that distinction where I feel a man deserves it. If you are simply going to award the half-point margin as a matter of course a man can win the first four rounds of an eight-round fight and the other fellow cannot win unless he does it inside the distance. There must be light and shade to it, some rounds where there is an extra reward to be gained. Abroad I find that hard to explain at times, although they deduct marks automatically in some places for butting or other offences.

Along with many other referees I do not like the present system where the referee's scores are announced after each contest. In the old days your card was sacrosanct and the crowd satisfied with finding the winner. Now they even bet on how a referee will make the score. If a referee has done something wrong the Board of Control will call him up fast enough and they should be the only people to see the way his arithmetic works out.

Now to the vexed question of referees' wages. I mention these because I know they must be of interest so many people ask about them. Well, let me say at once that no British referee is ever going to be a rich man from his boxing work, or even be able to make boxing his sole employment, far from it. While I do consider that there could be improvements, I am happy to feel our referees turn out for the love and enjoyment of the sport — I know I do and always have.

Even today if a referee has a British title fight he is lucky to receive £100 and is more likely to get about £60, while around the small halls the fees have not risen very much over the years. I might handle a dinner show, starting pretty late and finishing after midnight, travel in from Brentwood to Central London and receive about £25. In Europe British referees receive only expenses because on the Continent all the referees are amateurs, and although the fee for a world title fight in the United States has now been upped to 1,000 dollars you never come home with anything like that by the time you have paid your out-of-pocket expenses.

Of course I feel the fees for the man in the middle should be on a ratio to that received by the fighters. When I refereed Muhammad Ali's world heavyweight title defence against Brian London at Earls Court each boxer must have received more than £50,000. My fee was £300 which is still one of my best. The referee is very much a participant on the big occasions. He has to control the boxers, encourage them to do their best to entertain the public and keep an expert eye open for all aspects of safety. I have always felt that the top echelon of referees should be given a better deal, and then an even higher standard expected from them, because they are so important to the sport. I stress that this only applies at the very top so far as extra money is concerned. The small promotions often struggle and yet they are vital to boxing so no extra burden should be placed on them.

In recent years television money and backing from sponsors have made boxing a multi-million business, and it is in relation to this that the people who do the work should be considered. It applies to referees but, of course, to the boxers most of all — although from what I see and hear the top men are doing pretty well which is exactly correct.

One area in which the boys do suffer though is in advertising, or more specifically through the attitude of the TV companies to advertising. They refuse to allow boxers in British rings to wear even a small advertising motif on their shorts when the cameras are in action. They mutter something about moving adverts and then you switch on your set and see racing cars or rallying cars rattle around all over the screen simply plastered with adverts. Double standards? Of course. It is unfair to boxers — and remember a fighter is very much like a butterfly, he is not going to be around very long. A fighter at the top needs every available opportunity to earn, especially a lad who reaches a title chance after years of struggle and perhaps has only this one chance to cash in after all his service to the sport. It may be an old hobbyhorse but it is one well worth riding, and I hope there will soon be changes.

13

It's Always Great to Come Home

Funny geezer, this Harry Gibbs. Over the past few years I have been flown to some of the most exotic places in the world, seen so many wonderful sights that they are a jumble in my memory, and yet I can honestly say that the moment I touch down at my destination all I really want to do is go home. Remember, I was once taken on a trip just across the English Channel to France and did not get home for five years.

After saying that I have to acknowledge that I have been a remarkably fortunate chap. At the last count I had been to twenty-two countries, not counting the British Isles, and had refereed or judged at around forty world title contests. Then there were the trips to the Continent for European title fights and a variety of other excursions in answer to invitations to referee at major tournaments all over the place.

I have been lucky, too, because I have not had too many frights or adventures, although I do find air travel very boring when I am bound for somewhere on the other side of the globe like Japan or Korea and the plane is in the air for up to eighteen hours. Of course you cannot avoid the minor alarms, like losing my wallet and passport in Atlantic City, New Jersey, just as we were about to leave after John Conteh's disastrous world light-heavyweight title fight with Matthew Saad Muhammad. I was about to settle up at the hotel counter and join the British Press party on their trip to Maryland for Dave Green's world welter challenge to Sugar Ray Leonard when I realised my loss. I searched everywhere and so did the British Control Board general secretary Ray Clarke, who is often my travelling companion on long trips abroad. Nothing turned up and finally we set off dreading all the red tape that had to be cut before I could go home. When we reached the next stop it was Ray who solved the mystery. The wallet was safely in his bag. I had handed it to him as we packed, he had put it in his bag for safe keeping and then both of us had forgotten about it.

I will always remember the first time I flew back from Jamaica because it was far and away one of my worst flights. The plane developed some kind of engine problem and we put down at Montego Bay. All the transit lounges were packed and we could not leave the plane which was crowded out with Jamaicans, many of them children or youngsters heading for New York and jobs as au pairs. It was sweating hot, I was just about the only white person on the flight and all of us were very relieved when the engines were sorted out and once again we were up in the air. The BA girls had been rushing about all the time we were on the ground, but as soon as we went up again I was really proud of them. After all the heat and work, they appeared bright and fresh in clean white blouses, still dishing out orange juice to the kids as if the flight was only just starting off. I remember I sat next to a young Jamaican girl and she clutched my hand all the way to New York. She must have crossed herself a thousand times — in the end she almost had me frightened too!

In 1965 I made my first refereeing excursion outside Britain and struck lucky with a pleasant jaunt to Denmark and a show on an island at Aalborg. Al Phillips from London was the matchmaker and the promoter was Mogens Palle who has done so much to keep pro boxing alive in Denmark. The hospitality was great. Several British boys were on the bill along with the local heroes Tom Bogs and Jorgen Hansen, who went on to win the European welterweight title.

It was the first of several trips to Denmark, and in those early years I went to Stockholm in Sweden twice as well. On the second occasion I was lucky enough to referee Sonny Liston, then a former world heavyweight champion but still a formidable performer who left a deep impression on me. Sonny fought another American called Elmer Rush, and in the second round a bad cut opened under the ex-champ's eye. He always carried a scar there and it was such a deep one you could have dropped a half-crown into it. Out in Sweden they have no Board of Control to lay down what can be used on cut eyes and Liston's cornermen poured all kinds of stuff into that wound. Anyway, he did not delay them too long. He stopped the luckless Rush in a hurry. When you were in the ring you really felt his presence: his chest seemed as big as his shoulders, just for a start. He was made in depth, fearsome to look at but a gentleman in the ring. I explained the rules to him beforehand and there was little reaction from him, although he obeyed them without any problems.

In July 1968 I went on another trip in which Al Phillips, the Aldgate Tiger who was once the European feather-weight champion, was involved, only this time he was not as pleased with my refereeing as he had been in Denmark.

I was invited out to Kingston, Jamaica, to handle a Commonwealth lightweight title fight. Phillips's fighter, Love Allotey from Ghana, was defending against the Jamaican Percy Hayles. It was a hard contest, very close and I gave it to Hayles by a whisker. Al and I flew back to London on the same flight, one at the back, the other up front and we never exchanged a word all the way home.

The fee for the job was £500 — that seemed fine but I was not very heavily in pocket by the time I got home. What I did not know was that the fee had to meet all expenses apart from the return fare. Still, I enjoyed Jamaica and they must have liked me because in 1973 their Boxing Board invited me back.

Their intention was that I should referee the world heavyweight title clash between Joe Frazier, then the champion, and George Foreman, very much the up-and-comer with an unbeaten record and a frightening run of quick wins. I arrived in Kingston but did not get the job. The Americans took over and finally Arthur Mercante was appointed as referee. The Jamaicans paid me the same fee as he received for the world title and I handled another Commonwealth title match involving Percy Hayles. This time he defended the lightweight crown and stopped the Canadian Al Ford in twelve rounds with a badly damaged eye.

Foreman won the big one in two rounds, giving Frazier, who was too brave for his own good, a terrible beating. After the show I was in a restaurant with Mercante and a party that included several British writers when Arthur asked me in front of them all if I thought he had stopped the fight too late. It was embarrassing for me, but I told him that as he was asking my opinion I felt he had stepped in several punches too late because by then Frazier was a sitting target. Foreman had literally lifted him off the floor with his last big hit and by then Joe was defenceless. Arthur is a fine referee but that night he was slow.

The morning after the fight the new champion, Foreman, called a snap Press conference at the hotel where most of us were staying, and I nipped round to pass the word to Wal Bartleman of the Evening Standard. I knocked him up and Wal grabbed notebook and pen before rushing off ahead of me to be in time. He turned a corner and ran right into the hotel swimming pool, going in with quite a splash. Needless to say poor old Wal — one of the great characters of boxing writing — received scant sympathy from his colleagues. Reg Gutteridge, always a bloke with a quip to suit the occasion, made a comment I remember even now. Walter was just about the only one to tip the winner and Reg said 'Wally may be able to find the winner but he can't master walking on water just yet.'

Before the fateful Jamaican showdown I had never seen Foreman but I had heard a fair bit about him. Shortly before I went out I flew home from a European title fight in Switzerland with the famous promoter George Parnassus and he told me he expected Frazier to be beaten. In fact he reckoned Joe was daft to take on Foreman. George must have been at his peak at that time and it is hard to see how he allowed himself to be defeated so badly by Muhammad Ali in Zaire, although I suppose both the African climate and the psychological factors came into it. As always, Ali was a master when it came to psyching opponents and poor George seemed to fall for the whole bag of tricks, so far as one could tell from a distance.

As I settled in as a 'Star' referee in the sixties, I found myself commuting more and more often to Europe for world or European title contests. In December 1969 I went to Kiel in West Germany to referee a match to fill the vacant heavyweight championship of Europe. German Peter Weiland met Bernard Thebault of France for a title left vacant by our own Henry Cooper. Henry had survived a succession of low blows to stop Italy's Piero Tomasoni in Rome but then needed a cartilage operation and gave up the crown while he was having it. I was not put to any great test in Kiel because the German knocked Thebault out in the first round.

In a previous chapter I mentioned Scotland's world lightweight champion Ken Buchanan and I shall enlarge on Ken's career here because I remember him best for his adventures abroad. It was to judge Ken's first defence of the title that I made my very first trip to the United States, flying to California to see him face Ruben Navarro at the Sports Arena in Los Angeles. The man who should have met him was former world champion Mando Ramos but he pulled out three days before the fight, claiming a training injury, and Navarro came in as a substitute. Ken had taken the World Boxing Council's version of the light-weight crown by outpointing Ismael Laguna in San Juan, Puerto Rico, five months before, and his defence with Navarro in February 1971 earned him universal recognition at last.

The fight was a triumph for the lad from Edinburgh, wearing his tartan trunks with pride. He held off Navarro's early rush and from then on dominated the fight. I scored it to him 9-2 with four even, referee Mercante and judge Lee Grossman both made it 9-4 with two even. Next day one of the local papers, the Herald-Examiner, said: 'Buchanan is no European creampuff. He's a tough twenty-five-year-old boxer with a classic jab and a willingness to mix it whenever the gauntlet is thrown to see who has the most courage.' That summed up very accurately the way Buchanan approached his work. He was a man of remark-able ability, operating with pride and self-confidence.

At the ringside that night was a crowd of Scots, giving Ken plenty of vocal support, cheering him home from here to Limerick. They were waving a flag carrying the cross of St Andrew and were proper offended when a mob of Mexicans tried to take it off them. Now I dislike any kind of violence at the ringside but I must confess to a sneaking admiration for the way those lads looked after themselves. The Jocks really gave those Mexicans some stick.

Four years after the Los Angeles trip I travelled even further to judge yet another Buchanan world fight, this time an attempt to lift back the title from a smart Jap called Guts Ishimatsu. A lot of water had flowed under the lightweight bridge since the Navarro match. Buchanan was caught up in the politics always surging about the title scene and then beaten in thirteen rounds at Madison Square Garden by Roberto Duran. Finally, though, patience was rewarded and he went to Tokyo to bid for the World Boxing Council version of the title. By this time Ken was twenty-nine and although he was still the European champion he had possibly lost a little of his sharpness, at least at world level. He lost on points over fifteen rounds, retained the European crown five months later and announced his retirement. Since then he has returned with considerable success, just to underline what a remarkable fighter he is.

In Tokyo Ken suffered a black eye in training and should not really have fought, but he put up a fine performance and was never too far behind. In his corner that night was the London trainer Freddie Hill, yet another of those characters about whom so many tales are told it is hard to separate fact from fiction. Fred was there on the hurry-up, called up at the last moment to give Ken a hand. The blond Scot could hardly have picked on a bloke with more experience. Fred trained the Finnegans throughout their careers and in his time has prepared men like Alan Rudkin, Brian McCaffrey and Johnny Pritchett, all great warriors. Away from boxing Fred speaks his mind and is something of a comedian as well, as I discovered on the way back. The flight is a marathon trip and we had a bit of a party, taking up a whip to pay for the champagne, only Fred was skint because Buchanan did not pay him out until they were back in London.

We put Fred in the whip round, of course, and as I was holding the kitty it was me he came to when he wanted some fags out of it. I was in a playful mood by then and told him 'Sorry Fred, time for sleep, no fags.' He called me everything, and a Cockney can be very colourful with his turn of phrase when he concentrates. We all had a laugh, and then some kip. When we landed at Heathrow I reached up for my carrier bag only for a load of knives, forks and spoons to topple out. You should have seen the faces of the Japanese cabin crew who thought I was trying to nick them. We straightened it out and I was well aware who had landed me in it — it was the bold Fred getting his own back.

Buchanan was a truly extraordinary fighter. He boxed away from home more than any of our world champions I am sure. Indeed he never took part in a world title match in Britain. He relied on his own ability, acted as his own Board of Control and all round was one of the most exceptional performers we have produced since the war. Most champions, and I do not blame them, insist on playing at home whenever they can. In the case of Britain's champions they are wise because there is no Board like ours anywhere else in the world. In the United States every state has its own controlling body and they are all different, their rules widely divergent. Buchanan never worried about minor details like that. Denied major exposure in his own country, he chased the big purses wherever they were offered. He was a brilliant boxer, but a crowd pleaser too when it came to a punch-up. Just why he did not receive his proper recognition here I will never know, it is one of boxing's real mysteries.

The first time I refereed in Ghana I was amazed to face the largest crowd I had ever seen at boxing. When I went back again the attendance was even greater, around 125,000 is what the record books say. On each occasion the home fighter concerned was David 'Poison' Kotey and both fights were staged in Accra. The first contest was against a Japanese and I stopped it for Kotey halfway through. The ringside scene was truly amazing with the tribal chiefs decked up in their white robes, the moon looking huge hanging over the arena and the drums thudding away all the time. The fight was run under British rules with no judges and just myself to referee and find the winner. The Ghanaians can have had no objections because they stuck to that system for both contests.

The world featherweight title was at stake on each occasion and the second opponent was the American Danny 'Red' Lopez from Los Angeles. He not only gave Kotey one heck of a fight but took the decision as well. Kotey dominated early but then Lopez came on, boxing brilliantly. The crowd went mad at the end, but not with anger. They sang and roared but there was no invasion of the ring, in fact no trouble at all because they were so well disciplined. I was a very relieved man!

In 1979 I went back to Africa, only this time to Zambia for the Commonwealth light-heavyweight title match between the local hero Lottie Mwale and Gary Summerhays from Canada. The fight was staged in Lusaka before another huge crowd — although this time not all of them were paying customers by any means. Close to the stadium was a big hill and onto it packed literally thousands of people. They were a long way from the action but at least they did not have to pay.

It was another marvellous experience for me, right down to the entry of the tribal warriors before the start. In they came looking very much like the Zulus you see on the films and I must admit I jumped up in the ring out of the way. On the trip I even met the Zambian president Kenneth Kaunda and was impressed by the enthusiasm there is for boxing out there. In the fight itself Summerhays knocked Mwale down but the Zambian boy has a great deal of talent and fought his way back so well I stopped it in his favour in the end.

For me 1976 was a busy year for travelling. In May I refereed Esteban DeJesus in Puerto Rico before another huge crowd (he won on points), went to Tokyo in July and then out to Caracas in October. The Venezuelan trip was quite an experience, and it started with a scene that might have come straight out of a gangster movie. I flew into Caracas and was met at the airport. I was taken to a dingy-looking house and there was the promoter of the show lying on the bed being massaged. When it was brought to his attention that I was there he gave me a stare.

'Mr Gibbs,' he said, 'you have refereed nineteen world title fights.' I told him the record book was out of date and it was twenty-one. 'Well' he replied, 'I want you to know that Betulio is my boy.' I told him, 'Fine, and if he wins it he will get it.' With that he threw me the key to my room at the local Hilton Hotel. All he was doing was trying me out. The fight, incidentally, was a world fly-weight battle between the champion Miguel Canto and Betulio Gonzalez. It was presented in a bullring and hardly anyone turned up because it was pelting down with rain. The promoter had to go ahead because of tele-vision — and his boy was beaten as well.

A referee has to be ready for the call at any time. I was away on holiday in Spain when I was invited to Copen-hagen to handle the world middleweight title match be-tween the then champion Carlos Monzon from the Argen-tine and Denmark's Tom Bogs, both of whom have figured in this story before. The British Board had passed the message on, and I went to Barcelona to take the flight for Copenhagen. This time my wife Phyllis came along — after all she was on holiday too.

Bogs was in the fight up to the start of the fifth round but then Monzon began to crunch in hammer blows. He was thirty years old then but still a formidable puncher. First of all I gave Bogs a standing count and then a right put him down for another eight. The next Monzon move was a tricky one — and he was good at those. He half pushed Bogs down and tried to claim a stoppage win because his opponent had been over three times in one round. I whipped Bogs off the floor and indicated he had been pushed, but it was only prolonging the inevitable. Monzon soon floored him again and this time I did not bother to count but simply led the Dane back to his corner.

Monzon was a great character, the complete professional, and you will remember I had had an exchange of views with him when he fought Bouttier in Paris. He was at Wembley to watch his fellow-Argentinian Carlos Herrera challenge Maurice Hope for the world light-middleweight title, and when he saw me he wagged a finger at me with a grin. Clearly he remembered me showing him a finger of warning during the Bouttier fight when he pretended I had struck him.

Without a doubt one of the most remarkable fighters I have ever refereed is the Puerto Rican Wilfredo Gomez. First of all I saw him win on a count-out in Tokyo and then went to San Juan to referee him against the Mexican Carlos Zarate who was very much the King of Mexico at the time. It was a hectic fight from the start with the world bantam title at stake. The crowd soon got worked up and in one round they made so much noise no one heard the bell. When I realised — thanks to the lights going up — Gomez had thudded in a good punch before I could jump between them. Without the lights they would just have gone on battling. Zarate came out for the next round but with Gomez steaming on the Mexican corner soon slung in the towel. Pound for pound Gomez is one of the best I have seen, and since then he has kept on winning against featherweights and super-featherweights.

Another eventful night in San Juan came with the world welter fight between Wilfredo Benitez, the local boy, and Carlos Palomino from California, the man who lifted his title from our own John H. Stracey. A split decision went to Benitez and I made him the winner by three or four rounds. The referee had him even further in front but the second judge, the American referee Zach Clayton, put Palomino into the winner's slot. Afterwards even Palomino told Zach he must be crazy, or words to that effect, and he replied that the sun must have been in his eyes. Palo mino was a man I took to: his behaviour on his visits to London was first class, very friendly and easy, and he was a fighter with intelligence.

The night Benitez lost the title in Las Vegas I was once again in the judge's seat. He came unstuck against Sugar Ray Leonard, the former Olympic champion who has made the welterweight division even more lucrative than the heavyweights — and that says plenty for the charisma of this talented performer.

When our Fen Tiger Dave Green took him on in Landover, Maryland, Leonard smashed him out in four rounds. But the judges, once again including yours truly, finally did have a chance to perform when he figured in the record-breaking clash with Roberto Duran — yes, the same Panamanian warrior who once beat Buchanan for the lightweight crown. The pair of them pulled in more cash from one fight than any other couple, surpassing even Muhammad Ali and that took some doing.

The venue was Montreal and it was Duran who came away with the title. He stuck to the flashy Leonard like a limpet, refusing to allow him to dictate and finishing a clear winner. It was a fight that lived up to the pre-publicity and cried out for a return. When it came in New Orleans I was at Wembley watching Maurice Hope and Herrera but was able to see the fight on closed-circuit television. It was a disappointment, and it was Leonard who gave me the real let-down even though he finished up a sensational winner when Duran quit.

Sugar Ray had no need to copy Ali with his taunting and kidding. In fact he did more taunting than Ali ever did and I reckon the referee should have had a word or two in his ear. The Americans go for a bit of showbiz but they do not give points for dancing and insulting. If I had been in charge I would, naturally, have given him some leeway and then a caution or two. But here in Britain we call what he was up to ungentlemanly conduct. Leonard might well have used similar antics in the Montreal fight but then Roberto never gave him a chance. He was always too close, too much in the middle of the action. In New Orleans he looked more and more nonplussed; he knew he was away from home and being made to look a fool. He seemed to me thoroughly disgusted, convinced Leonard had everything going for him, and that may well have been why he jacked it in.

When it comes to heavyweights I have refereed many fine contests, but I have missed out on one or two of the big ones. As I told you, Frazier-Foreman eluded me despite the Jamaican Boxing Board flying me in for the job, and Ali-Frazier went the same way, even after I went to the Philippines at the invitation of the Frazier camp. This was the third meeting between these two great champions, the score was 1-1 and this time it was Ali defending the crown. It was billed as 'The Thriller in Manila' and that proved an apt slogan.

Since Frazier fought Joe Bugner in London he had had a change of manager. Yank Durham, the man who guided him from the start, died suddenly, with Eddie Futch, one of the best trainers in the game, taking over. It was Eddie who sent the telegram to London asking for me to go out and when I took the Jumbo jet at Heathrow I went fully expecting to handle the fight. The second day in Manila I was approached in the hotel lobby by a fellow I am sure was with the Muhammad Ali camp. He asked me if I was doing the fight and I said I thought so. Then he put the 64,000 dollar question: 'What would I do if the champ kept on holding?' Ali was a past master at holding and I told the bloke he could expect the same treatment as a six-rounder back in Britain. Two warnings and then, very likely, out he would go. 'I don't think you will get the fight' he said — and he was right. I missed out, but then so did the Americans they had out there. The Philippine president insisted on one of his own men handling it and the kid who stepped in, Carlos Padilla, did a very good job I thought.

The fight itself was the best heavyweight combat I have ever seen, a terrific battle and up to the tenth round there was nothing in it. Frazier kept going forward. He took a lot of stick, but then Ali absorbed plenty too. Frazier gave everything but just fell short. After fourteen rounds Eddie Futch shook his head sadly and the corner pulled Joe out on his stool. I will never know if Ali was kidding when he collapsed on the canvas when he realised that Frazier was not coming out for the final three minutes. He may be the greatest showman of them all but he must have been close to exhaustion too after fourteen rounds like those.

The arguments about who is the greatest heavyweight of them all are part of the spice of boxing. I have always had great admiration for Rocky Marciano, but so many people have so many theories. The man who impressed me most at close quarters was Liston, even though his best days were over when I refereed him. He was a fearsome machine. I did not watch his two fights with Ali, of course; I have only seen them on television and read about them, but to me they constitute a mystery. I am sure that goes for many other people, and the Muhammad Ali reign certainly got off to a strange start — for all its charisma later on.

Old Big 'Ed

It may seem presumptuous, but then I do not care. Before I wind up this epistle I would like to hand out a few Harry Gibbs Awards, only verbal ones of course but based on my years of enjoyment in boxing all over the world.

The award to the best pound-for-pound fighter I have seen goes to the Puerto Rican Wilfredo Gomez, while any award for the man who has had most effect on the sport must go to Muhammad Ali — although that was a bad effect in the twilight of his career when he continued fighting much too long.

In British boxing I would strike a special award for Bruce Woodcock. I did not referee him, of course, but I regarded him as one of our greatest hopes for a world heavyweight title and I am sure he would have become champion if he had not been put in against Tami Mauriello too soon. Dave Charnley should step up for an award in the pound-for-pound department while my award for sportsmanship in the ring would go to Chris Finnegan. His behaviour after I named Johnny Frankham the winner over him in their first fight was exemplary. His acceptance of the decision was a lesson to all professionals, and on that night it also defused a potentially explosive situation.

British professional boxing is in a healthy state and one of the main reasons is the way the Board of Control exercises its authority. Of course they take plenty of stick — all controlling bodies do because it is impossible to please everyone — but they are streets ahead of any other national commission in the world, at least from my experience and I have been to a heck of a lot of places.

The Board is strict about medical rules and reports, indeed about all the many safeguards vital to the sport. The Board members are not financially involved and that is important, yet most have many years of experience in boxing to assist them in their decisions. I am not currying favour with the Board either — I have only a few years to go anyway — but I know the system works and British boxers receive the very best treatment possible. I suppose respect is the operative word because those in authority do have a great respect for the boxers under their care.

I would like to see proper worldwide control based as far as possible on the British system, but that is a near impossibility. It suits too many people to have a World Boxing Council and a World Boxing Association and play off one against the other for there ever to be agreement on just one world organisation.

My years in boxing have been packed with excitement and never more so than in the last few years when Britain has become a major power in world boxing, as Ken Buchanan, John Stracey, Jim Watt, Alan Minter, John Conteh and Maurice Hope have proved already, and several more may well have done even before this book is published. In putting down a few memories of my life I am sure my own love of boxing has come through. There are still a few places left in the world where a man can prove himself a man and one of them is the boxing ring. He does not need simply strength, fitness and ability; he must have courage and self-control, sportsmanship and a sense of compassion too. It is a hard sport, but it produces a camaraderie like no other, and I have never regretted becoming involved since the first day I handed over my 3d subscription at the Oxford and Bermondsey Club.

Whatever I am now is conditioned by all that has happened to me and, apart from the wasted years in the prison camps, there is very little that I regret. In Bermondsey as a kid I grew up amongst some wonderful people. Times may have been hard but I enjoyed a family life that was second to none and my Dad and Mum, Gus and Nellie, did a great job for us all. They put me right on so many things, and old Dr Stansfield's boys' clubs taught me so many more. Club spirit meant a great deal to most of the lads at the Oxford and Bermondsey and I would like to think it was as strong today. Sadly I doubt if it is. All club spirit really meant was following a set of principles laid down by the club leaders and being loyal both to the club and to the other members.

After the war and my own boxing career came the years as an amateur trainer. The best of those were spent with the Belsize Club; there I was privileged to work with men who are the nearest thing I have met to true Corinthians. It was one of the best periods of my life — eventful and humorous. The Belsize attitude is completely amateur. The sport and the fun it brings are all that matter, but in a way the Belsize members have a great deal in common with the administrative stewards of the Board of Control. They may control a professional sport but they, too, are Corinthians in their own way.

Sadly, the overall attitude of amateur boxing's top officials towards the professional side of the sport is lamentable. I feel it is out of touch with the vast majority of amateur boxers, too, because I will take a bet that most of them dream that one day they will wear a Lonsdale Belt proudly as a British professional champion and go on to win a world title. I look forward to a day, far off I am afraid, when the two sides of the sport work together, particularly on the medical and general safety aspects. To do so is only commonsense after all.

If I have a regret, it concerns the Lonsdale Belt. This is the most magnificent individual trophy in sport in my view, especially when you consider that the same trophy goes to every man to win a British title and then he keeps it as his own when he has emerged victorious from three title contests in a particular weight. When I watch the champions being handed their Belts I feel a pang of regret because I would dearly have loved to win one myself. Otherwise no regrets at all. I have not earned a fortune but my house is paid for, the car — solid British of course — is mine and I have my family around me.

Life in the docks, too, has shaped my life, helped me to form opinions and taught me much that has guided my approach to refereeing I am sure. Perhaps my time in dockland sums up best what I like about Britain and being British. I am a Conservative, a royalist too, and all those years I have held a minority view in the docks I am certain. Yet I have been able to stand up for what I believe in and still work alongside some of the best blokes you will find anywhere. That is my idea of freedom, and another reason why whenever I am on my travels abroad I am always happy to come home.

Boxing has brought me so much pleasure, so many experiences; but none of them compare with the day I went to Buckingham Palace to receive the OBE from Her Majesty the Queen. Never mind about world championships, that was the greatest honour and the greatest day of my life. 'For services to boxing.' Well, I am not the one to say if I deserved it but I know just how much I enjoyed receiving it.

First of all I got a letter, and it crossed my mind it might be one of the lads at work pulling my leg. I was in bed after a late shift when it came but when I checked the official seal on it I was convinced it was the genuine article. I sat there amazed, just looking at it, and then read it over and over again. The letter gives no hint of what honour you are going to receive. It simply says that the Prime Minister has it in mind to recommend you.

In the end it turned out to be the OBE, or Other Bugger's Efforts as some of the comedians would tell you. Anyway I had some frustration finding out exactly what the honour was. They were not mentioned on television the day I thought they were being announced, and on New Year's Day there were no papers either. Anyway, that was soon sorted out and then came the wait, and the preparations, for the trip to the Palace.

Phyllis and our daughter Sheila formed the escorting party — Sheila was determined to make it even though she was pregnant with young Matthew at the time and due the day of the Investiture ceremony. She came along, enjoyed the day and then produced the baby the very next morning. I asked her mother what would have happened if anything had started at the Palace. 'Well' she replied, 'instead of calling him Matthew we would have called him Buckingham.'

The day of the ceremony I was really on edge. You know me, royalist through and through, but I will admit I was very nervous. Very proud too, and you will never find me handing the award back, they would have to come and drag it off me by force. It simply had to be a morning coat job and I went off looking like an undertaker. Not really though, and I felt it had to be done right for such an important occasion.

When the Queen handed the award to me I spent some time with her. She was well briefed about my activities in boxing and she inquired what I was doing for my full-time living. So she heard a bit about the docks too. I went home walking on air but I soon came down to earth again, the lads made sure of that. I turned up at work the next day to find my OBE recorded on a huge placard above my desk. 'Old Big 'Ed' it said — just the dockers' way of making quite sure I wasn't too carried away by my own importance.